The Problem of Good:
Finding Purpose Amid the Chaos of Reality

Richard P. Mullin

AllrOneofUs Publishing
Baltimore, Md & Huntsville, Al

THE PROBLEM OF GOOD: FINDING PURPOSE AMID THE CHAOS OF REALITY

First edition. April 9, 2022.

ISBN: 979-8201503758

Written by Richard Mullin.

Table of Contents

To Marian.

Special thanks to Mike Susko, who encouraged and guided me through the publication process.

Many members of the Society for the Advancement of American Philosophy have helped me immensely through their writings and conversations.

I also thank the many students at St. Bernard College in Alabama, and Wheeling Jesuit University from whom I learned at least as much as I taught.

And finally, thanks to NovOntos for the use of his cover art, "Emerging Leaves."

Chapter 1:
Purposefulness
in a Materialist Age

Materialism and Teleology

We can look at the things around us and the events in our own lives in several ways, but two of them stand out. We can look back at the causes, or look ahead to the purpose. For example, we may compare a tree that a storm knocks over to a baseball that a centerfielder throws to home-plate. In the first case, air moves from an area of higher pressure to one of lower pressure in ways that meteorologists can explain. A tree or house that happens to be in the path of the wind might be destroyed, but the destruction does not serve any known purpose. By contrast, the trajectory of the baseball results from the fielder's intention to get the ball to home-plate before the base-runner. Explainable factors such as the skill and strength of the player, wind resistance, and gravity all play a role in the outcome of when and where the throw ends. But, unlike the storm, the throw occurs only because of the intention of the player. Some people believe *everything* happens for a purpose. "It was (or wasn't) meant to be." Others hold that apart from human intentions, such as throwing a baseball, nothing has a purpose. We might also believe that there is purpose in the universe but that not everything serves a purpose.

Examining the meaning of purpose, we may ask, "Why are we here?" This question might refer to an immediate presence such as why are we here in this meeting, classroom, or social get-together; or it may address a more cosmic concern: "Why are we here on this planet? Why do we exist?" Looking backwards in the case of the specific "here," we may say that we are here because we were called in by our boss, it was on our class schedule, or we were invited. If we are extremely literal minded, we may say that we are here because we drove or walked. Those answers look backwards at how we got here. But we may also look ahead to the purpose of our presence: to discuss how to improve our company's safety record, to gain insight into an academic field, or to be introduced to a method of enhancing our income by selling home products. Our individual purpose might be different from that of the boss, professor, or host. But whether the purpose is that of the person who called us to be there, or our purpose for showing up, the purpose refers to looking ahead to what we expect from our action of attending.

In asking the larger question of why we are here in the sense of our very existence, we may again look backwards. Depending on our knowledge and interest we may begin with the "big bang" and trace the history of star and planet generations up to and including the evolution of life on earth. Or we may be more interested in demographics, genealogy, or how our parents met. All of these questions look backwards and involve research in physical or social science or family history. But the question that emerges as most important to each of us asks, "Now that we are here, what should we do with our lives, what is our purpose for living?" We might try to answer this question by believing that we are part of a larger purpose and that we need to find our individual role. Or we might believe that our purpose consists only in what we ourselves create in an otherwise purposeless universe.

The belief that all events can be explained completely and solely by what has happened previously is called a materialist or mechanistic view. These terms reflect an older worldview that portrayed nature as composed of material particles moving according to the laws of mechanical science.[1] But contemporary materialists think in terms of every kind of physical energy and even allow for some randomness. Purpose plays no role.

The view that things happen for a purpose we call a "teleological" view. This word is based on the Greek word *telos,* which refers to an end or purpose. Of course, a person may believe that physical causes—pushing from behind, and teleological causes—pulling from ahead, may both be factors. The belief that there is some purpose in nature, however little, marks a decisive contrast to the materialist world-view. The distinction between materialism and purpose goes back at least to the time of Plato.[2] The following two sections will contrast the traditional teleological view with the prevailing contemporary materialist view.[3]

Purpose and the Meaning of Good

From at least the time of Aristotle, the Good was identified with purpose.[4] Aristotle's *Nicomachaen Ethics* opens with the assertion: "Every art and every inquiry, and similarly every action and pursuit, is thought to aim at some good; and for this reason, the good has been declared to be that at which all things aim."[5] The highest good is the end, *telos,* which is desired for its own sake. The task of ethics consists in understanding what this good is and how to attain it.

Aristotle's notion of the Good as the final end or purpose came into Medieval Christian thought primarily through the work of St. Thomas Aquinas and his theory of natural law. St. Thomas defined natural law as an aspect of eternal law, the order by which all things are directed to their end.[6] Like Aristotle, St. Thomas thought of God as pure being - pure actuality, whereas creation consisted of a process of things *becoming* by actualizing their potential. Using a popular example, an acorn has the potential to become a mature oak tree. Inanimate things, plants, and non-rational animals achieve their actuality naturally. We humans, as rational beings, participate in the eternal law and must seek our end voluntarily using reason and free will.

Reason and free will, in this view, constitute the human faculties that enable us to know and love that which is good. Goodness and being are co-extensive, meaning that all being is good. Evil is a lack of something that ought to be. To take an example of a physical evil, if a person loses his eyesight, we call that a physical evil, (more often we would say "misfortune") because we cherish sight as a good thing that ordinarily accompanies our human nature. Moral evil consists of a lack of virtue. As we humans grow from infancy to adulthood, we *ought* to learn to control our lives by reason. The habits of rational governance constitute virtues such as temperance, courage, and justice. Anyone who fails to develop these qualities slips into intemperance, cowardice, and injustice. Since being is good, a good human being is one who is constantly *becoming* more human, which means a more highly developed rational animal. As we develop in this way, we actualize our potential and move toward achieving our end, our *telos*.

Contemporary Evolutionary Materialism

Contemporary materialism provides a view that rejects all the concepts that constitute traditional natural law theory. Materialists deny the reality of the soul, eternal law, teleology, and objective good. Francis Crick states the materialist position in explicit contrast to the notion of a soul, which his wife had learned in Catholic school:

> The Astonishing Hypothesis is that "You," your joys and your sorrows, your memories and your ambitions, your sense of personal identity and free will, are in fact no more than the behavior of a vast assembly of nerve cells and their associated molecules. [7]

If this thesis holds true, then we must understand conscious behavior of human organism as nothing but a product of physical and chemical events at the level of molecules.

For contemporary materialist thought, the term "soul" does not refer to anything real. The activities that traditional philosophy attributed to the soul are now seen as nothing but "the behavior of nerve cells and other molecules." So, it is not you and I who experience joy and sorrow, remember things past, and strive for things future––the molecules are doing all of this.

Reason itself does not have the privileged place that it had in traditional thought, but we can choose to make it a supreme value. The materialist philosophers and scientists, to their credit, or to the credit of their molecules, give reason a place of pre-eminence. Materialist philosopher Daniel Dennett says in praise of scientific researchers and in response to those who argue that "trading mystery for mechanism" will impoverish our view of human potential:

> Look around at those who are participating in this quest for further scientific knowledge and eagerly digesting the new discoveries; they are manifestly not short on optimism, moral conviction, engagement in life, commitment to society.[8]

Fortunately, *we* can value such things as life, health, and virtue. But *nature* is indifferent, neither good nor bad apart from our judgments. For materialism, there can be no eternal law, and inanimate objects do not seek ends. The question for us is whether we can show that the principle of seeking ends still applies to us humans as understood in contemporary science.

To answer this question, we must first look at what the materialists put in the place of the teleology of eternal law, namely, an interpretation of *natural selection* based on chance. In the materialist view, everything from the formation of molecules to the most complex human thought comes about by natural selection. Some molecules replicate themselves and therefore copies of them will survive. Of the replicating molecules, the ones that are best suited to the environment in which they find themselves and which are not self-destructive, will pass along copies of themselves. This process continues as some of the molecules happen to join with others to form more complex structures. The fittest of these survive and eventually evolve into living organisms, which by the same process of natural selection develop sensation, consciousness, and intelligence. In the materialist view, there is no need to posit a design or goal at any point in the process. At the lower levels there is no striving or wanting to survive. At the level of consciousness, the desire to survive might give an organism a competitive edge, allowing those organisms who happen to have a survival instinct to survive and reproduce. At the level of intelligence, planning and deliberately working toward long-range goals may greatly enhance survival.

Daniel Dennett offers an explanation of free will based on non-biological survival structures called *memes*. *Memes* are described as "cultural replicators" parallel to genes, which are the biological replicators. Examples of *memes* would be anything that is part of what we call our culture, from the way we prepare food to the way we enjoy music. The *memes* are products of natural selection so that, for instance, an innovation in food or music may or may not be replicated depending on whether it is to the liking of the biological host.

Just as our genes have a natural tendency to replicate themselves, so do our cultural memes. Dennett quotes Richard Dawkins author of *The Selfish Gene* and coiner of the term "meme." Dawkins writes:

> *We* have the power to defy the selfish genes of our birth and
> if necessary the selfish memes of our indoctrination...We are
> built as gene machines and cultured as meme machines but
> we have the power to turn against our creators. We alone on
> earth can rebel against the power of the selfish replicators.[9]

Who are "we?" We are sharers of information. With the sharing of *memes* we have the beginning of a community rather than just an aggregate of individuals. The question is how we rebel against the replicators as Dawkins affirms that we in fact do. Dawkins does not say how, and so Dennett himself attempts to answer this question. The answer is that the *memes* open up a world of imagination, which provides a variety of options to choose from. Because of imagination we are not limited to only the option that best enhances our own individual survival, nor the survival of our genes. One person may forgo a family and children to live a life of service; another may do so to live a life of hedonistic delights. In both cases the genes' metaphorical "desire" for perpetuation will not be met.

There does not seem to be any reason in the nature of things to affirm that any choices are better than any others. And although scientific thinkers like Dennett and Dawkins stand poles apart from the classical existentialists who hold that reality is absurd, the ultimate outlook on what is good or bad is strangely similar. As Jean-Paul Sartre states after arguing that values have no reality apart from the choice of a free being who chooses them:

> It follows that my freedom is the unique foundation of values and that *nothing,* absolutely nothing, justifies me in adopting this or that particular value, this or that particular scale of values.[10]

And yet, it seems that those who pursue scientific knowledge, as well as other pursuits such as health-care or social justice, do so with the assumption that they are on to something real. We need to ask whether our contemporary scientific world-view is compatible with the notion that science is really good and not just one of the myriad of memes, along with such things as astrology and sorcery, that people happen to adopt.

Evolutionary Teleology

Our view of reality can go beyond materialism and therefore be literally a *meta-physical* view. However, it is not necessary to posit an ontological break between nature and super-nature; what we need may be a larger understanding of nature. Developing a larger view begins with a critique of the materialist view.

The materialist view is non-falsifiable. Whatever happens is known after the fact to be possible. Since this world is what it is, and since according to materialist doctrine natural selection is the only way that things develop, a world like this could have and must have evolved by natural selection. Likewise, since there is such a thing as consciousness, according to the materialistic hypothesis, consciousness obviously could and did evolve by natural selection. Given the vastness of time and space, anything that can happen probably will.

The question is whether the materialist view is the most rational one, as materialists assume it is. A non-materialist view holds that consciousness precedes evolution and so evolution is consciousness struggling toward more complete manifestations. Those who affirm a God-Creator, or hold to pantheism, or any form of idealism, see consciousness as a reality prior to matter. I will refer to those who hold a non-materialists view as teleologists, meaning that they believe that life is purposeful. Teleologists take consciousness as a given and can examine the development of consciousness in human beings without appeal to a miracle. In using the term "miracle" in this context, I am not making any super-naturalist assumptions, but am referring to any event that is wonderful, surprising, and not understood.[11] The materialist view holds that the evolution of consciousness is the product of unconscious particles that over time become conscious. The emergence of consciousness would seem to be a miracle, although a very slowly forming one. But materialists do not see the need for a miracle because they take consciousness for granted. The bland assumption of consciousness resembles the way that we as individuals look at our own personal consciousness. We do not consider our consciousness and the control that we have over our voluntary muscles as a miracle, because by the time we are mature enough to think about these things, they have already become so familiar as to seem ordinary.

The familiarity of consciousness is seen in the fact that it is difficult to speak of the movement of material elements toward unity without using the language of intention. In materialist descriptions the elements "strive," they are "selfish," they "tend." Materialists make it clear enough that this language is metaphorical and that the elements do not really have intentions. I think most of us frequently miss a most crucial gap in our knowledge, namely that the workings of anything below the conscious level lies beyond our understanding. We think we understand inanimate nature because of familiarity and because of analogy to intentionality. Even when we manipulate things through our science and technology, it is our intentions that we understand, not the inner working of the things.

Both the materialists and the teleologists struggle with the relation between the elements and consciousness. The materialists explain the *whole,* namely human consciousness as a more complicated rendition of the mechanical action of the parts; genes are complicated molecular replicators, and *memes* are the cultural equivalent of biological genes. Can we instead turn the relationship around and see the movement of the parts as primitive expressions of the reality that we experience at the human level? Might there be a force which American Philosopher C. S. Peirce at the turn of the 20th century calls *agape,* meaning love, working alongside of mechanical necessity and chance?

Pierce holds a view, which he calls *agapaism,* which affirms a force of loving attraction that moves things at every level toward a teleological unity.[12] In this case evolutionary attraction would be seen as a more primitive instance of what we would think of as the highest form of love. Agapaism is the inverse of materialism in that it gives the movement toward meaningful unity an ontological priority rather than seeing it as a mere chance product of inert particles. This view is not provable, but it is *at least as feasible* as the materialist view.

Faith and Reason

The idea of teleology brings up the specter of God, which the materialists find abhorrent. They do so because they associate God with faith, and faith with blind trust and apostasy to reason. Dawkins, after defining faith as "blind trust," writes:

> The meme for blind faith secures its own perpetuation by the simple unconscious expedient of discouraging rational inquiry... Blind faith can justify anything. If a man believes in a different god, or even if he uses different rituals for worshipping the same god, blind faith can decree that he should die--on the cross, at the stake, skewered on a Crusader's sword, shot in a Beirut street, or blown up in a bar in Belfast. Memes have their own ruthless way of propagating themselves. This is true of patriotic and political as well as religious blind faith. [13]

Dawkins convicts faith as the apostasy to reason, and as the generator of much of the violence and evil in human history.

The notion that faith excludes reason runs contrary to the traditional notion of Natural Law that requires that we strive to "know the truth about God." Natural law requires believers to think rationally about God, a task which thinkers such as Dawkins believe constitutes

a self-contradiction. Can a 21st century person accept the method and content of science and still affirm a non-materialist view of reality? This question is a paraphrase of the question that Josiah Royce asked in 1913: "In what sense, if any, can the modern man consistently be, in creed, a Christian?" [14] Our intention here is to go beyond Christianity, as Royce also did, to include any non-materialist view. Royce's answer to this question will be the subject of a later chapter, but for now we can begin to answer the question whether we can be scientific without being materialistic by looking closely at evolution.

Evolution seems to be a trial-and-error attempt toward a teleological unity. Is this *seeming* teleology a reality or an illusion? How can we think of the process beginning? Pure nothingness is incomprehensible. Of course, we can think of "nothing" between particles or beyond the expanding universe. But in these cases, we think of "nothing" juxtaposed to something. But what if nothing-at-all, neither God nor nature, existed? We can say the words but can have no comprehension of such hypothetical situations of nothingness. Fortunately, we *can* think of a material world, composed of elementary particles, whether it is created or non-created. Finding language that describes reality below human consciousness poses a problem as daunting as describing reality above the level of our consciousness. We can come closest by means of analogies, metaphors, and stories about the things that we can understand.

We can imagine the world beginning in a chaos of brute facts. Is this what reality was right before or right after the *big bang*? Such a concept of brute facts would be nightmarish and perhaps would constitute the terror and horror of some forms of psychosis. But what if there is a redeeming *agape*-love at work amid the chaos of brute facts? How long would it take to create a world with intelligent life? Is that what is happening as we speak? If so, how far along are we?

Evolution and Natural Law

Evolution is a movement away from the chaos of brute facts toward a conscious universal community. We can at last come to the seeds of a contemporary Natural Law theory. In the thirteenth century, St.

Thomas defined eternal law as "the order by which all things are directed to their end." We can interpret this statement in a way infinitely richer than he could since he was limited to a pre-Copernican world-view. We can see the "order" to which all things are directed as the teleological harmony to which the brute elemental facts are being called. An understanding of the "order" must include a theory of evolution, which needs not be limited to the materialist interpretations of some contemporary Darwinists.

The principle that genetically brought about the replications of molecules becomes conscious in us. The struggle against the separateness of brute facts is the reason that we are here. The same struggle gives us a purpose and direction in which we can progress. The four main precepts of traditional natural law are as pertinent as ever:

1. Preserve yourself, 2. Preserve your species, 3. Know the truth about ultimate reality, and 4. Create social justice.

The first three of these are easily understood. Self-preservation means that we strive to maintain and enhance our individual physical and psychological integrity. Preservation of our species means that we follow Dawkins's "selfish genes" to perpetuate the human race. Materialists and teleologists agree we should strive to know the ultimate nature of reality, although they disagree extremely on what this means. As for social justice, the materialist might see it as one meme among countless others; a teleologist more likely sees social justice as the goal of evolution.

Social justice can be described as an arrangement of practices that would allow for both freedom and unity. Evolution is working to overcome separateness and integrating all into community. Natural Law enjoins us to take part in that enterprise of creating such a community. But social justice cannot survive in a unity based on tyranny or conformity. Rather, justice would further the evolutionary process by allowing as much freedom as possible for each. *Anything that would hinder any person from evolving to his or her full potential, whether the hindrance is oppression, deliberate exclusion, marginalization, or neglect, would stand out as injustice.*

The conscious movement toward a just community would constitute the culmination of the whole process of evolution from the absolute chaos of brute facts. If the freedom and unity were universal, it would constitute what Josiah Royce called the "Great Community" and the "Beloved Community." Our purpose here is not to describe a Utopia but to imagine what we could be at our best. What is the ontological status of such an idea? To some extent it already exists. We have a degree of freedom and a degree of unity. Many of us (probably anyone reading this) can actualize our potential and do not suffer oppression, exclusion, or marginalization. Tragically, far too many people suffer these life choking evils, and are cut off from any sense of community. And even for those who are better off, the freedom and communal connectedness falls short of what we think it ought to be.

Purpose in Evolution: All or Nothing?

The argument today, at least in the popular culture, seems to contrast those who believe that the universe proceeds from an Intelligent Designer to those who attribute it to blind chance. The argument for the blind chance position holds that the process of evolution bears no resemblance to what would be the work of an Intelligent Designer. This argument takes the form of the classical atheist argument based on the problem of evil. If there were a good and almighty and all wise God as Creator, the world would be a lot nicer. But the universe is not a very nice place. The second premise bears a lot of weight. The world does not look like the product of a good Creator. While things are messy and violent on earth, the ancients, even up to the time of Immanuel Kant in the eighteenth century thought that at least the heavens reflected a rational order. We know now that, in the heavens, whole galaxies are colliding into each other and on earth the development of life is "red in tooth and claw."[15]

One response to the denial of a clean product from a good Creator with a clear purpose is to reject the notion of good, creation, and purpose, and posit a world that emerges by blind chance. Many if not most of the materialists hold this position as their main premise. They appeal to the notion that in the vastness of time and space an infinite number of universes evolve and ours happens to have beings with life, consciousness, and a degree of intelligence. This idea seems to have worked its way into the popular culture where characters on TV and movies casually mention alternative universes.

Does logic force us to accept the notion that only blind chance could have produced our world? I intend to offer an interpretation that diverges radically from the materialist views that effectively deny the significance of consciousness.[16] This chapter concludes with a sketch of the position that will be elaborated and applied in the remaining eleven chapters. Many instructional books on learning the *art of drawing* advise the budding artist to begin with a sketch to set the boundaries and proportions of the subject. Afterward, the details, accents, and shading can be applied to flesh out the picture. I will follow this pattern by giving a sketch of my proposal. Any attempt to explain reality, whether attempted by a philosopher, a theologian, or a physicist, must involve at least a little hubris. Honesty requires Platonic humility, which means that we call our ideas "a likely story," or in the words of Charles Sanders Peirce, "A guess at the riddle."

As a minimum requirement, a worldview must be possible, meaning that it exhibits both logical consistency and compatibility with known facts. The writer must then show that the view presented is probably true and at least as feasible, or more so, than other alternatives.

We begin with the recognition of brute facts, which constitute chaos and apparently no sign of any kind of consciousness, order, or benevolence. This statement applies to the period following the "big bang," to the development of stars and planets, and to the evolution of life on earth from the first protozoa to the "origin of species," and even to the history of the human race. The fundamental particles seem to be inert unconscious, impenetrable, and determined by the conflicting blind forces of both *necessity* and *chance*. They do not display completely random behavior, but follow a regularity that scientists discern as laws of physics.[17] Yet, their behavior also displays some randomness and uncertainty.[18] Moving from fundamental particles to biology, the forces of chance and necessity are still at work. The whole premise of evolution rests on the notion that random mutations occur but then become genetically fixed. This description does not go beyond the reality of brute facts although the elements become entangled in patterns that give rise to consciousness and the ability to find patterns and study them scientifically.

But we human beings, at this stage of our evolution have the ability to discern something different from brute facts. We experience *beauty*: in each other, in nature, in music and art, in our own creative ideas, and in scientific theories. We see enough order and what we call by the name of goodness to make many believe that a Creator-God is at work. This form of consciousness constitutes my title phrase, "the problem of good." Just as atheists deem the "problem of evil" as proof of God's non-existence, those who believe in a spiritual reality may see "the problem of good" as a challenge to materialism.

Of course, the materialists will pass all of this off as illusion, or at best, a quirk of a particular set of random mutations in our brain. The dogma of materialism holds that whatever we cannot understand at this stage of our evolution, meaning anything that does not fit the method and content of science, does not exist. With a relatively high level of intelligence, scientists can describe objectively the movement of elementary particles and energy. The assumption of popular materialism holds that the consciousness by which we know physical nature must be a product of nature as we know it.

In posing the problem of consciousness and matter, the danger of a simplistic all-or-nothing dualism looms. A person might think that we must choose between materialism and a kind of creationism. But the complexity and depth of reality should cause us to reject both religious and scientific fundamentalism. A person can reject a literal interpretation of the Bible, in fact reject the whole Bible, without being a materialist. Likewise, a person can reject materialism without being biblical fundamentalist.

An alternative vision sees the universe as a process of moving from absolute chaos to a cosmos that expresses order, beauty, harmony, consciousness, freedom, joy, and love. We *may agree* with the materialists that these qualities are subjective and fleeting, *but we need not agree*. We can rationally maintain that these qualities are prior to our known world and that they are powerful, creative, and productive. Whatever is the source of these qualities––call it God or don't––we may rationally maintain that evolution consists of these powers overcoming the chaos, necessity, and inertness of the elemental brute facts. To the extent that this vision is true, the qualities such as consciousness, freedom, love, and creativity, which we experience to a degree in our own lives, have their seeds in the very formation of the universe.

Can we posit a chaos of blind, inert, purposeless, and brutal realities tending toward further chaos and division, and also a Creator Spirit working in the whole development of the universe including human evolution on earth to bring about purpose, intelligence, freedom and cooperation? To affirm both does not mean a dualism of two layers, one material and the other spiritual. Rather, the world itself reflects the interaction of the two opposing forces. In the pages to follow, I will elaborate on this interpretation and argue that it stands out as the most rational view we can hold.

Chapter 2:
The Pitilessness of Nature and the Problem of Good

Facing the Facts of Evolution

Any view of reality worthy of belief takes account of the facts that confront human beings in every aspect of our individual and communal lives, aspects such as those studied by natural science, social science, and history. These disciplines do not tell us where we should go from here, or how to get there, but they form the basis for understanding how we arrived at our present state of reality. The present discussion will focus on the facts revealed by science. Since 1859, when Darwin published his *Origin of Species,* the notion of evolution has impacted not only biology but also philosophy, theology, politics, and economics. Nothing in our intellectual life has been the same.

The working title of this book had been *Our Materialistic Age and the Problem of Good.* The use of the phrase "Our materialistic age" flows from the prevailing interpretation of Darwin. In this interpretation, there is no longer a need to deal with the problem of evil, a problem that vexed those who believed in a good and almighty Creator. Now, the things that we call evil are seen as simply things that we do not like, as an animal in the jungle does not like being eaten up by a predator. But the plight of the prey and our plight constitute the same process of evolution, which is blind and indifferent to the fate of all of us beasts. The problem that we must encounter is "the problem of good," beginning with whether there is such a thing as good, beyond the enjoyment that an animal or human predator takes in eating its meal, finding its mate, or other such pleasures. This investigation must be undertaken in the context of Darwinian evolution.

Is Anything Really Good?

The question that defines this chapter and this whole book is whether the term "good" refers to an objective reality rather than to merely a subjective point of view as when a big fish eats a little fish—The big fish likes it, the little fish doesn't. Theologians use the term *theodicy,* which literally means the justification of God, to describe the problem of believing in a good God in an evil universe. *Theos* means God, *dike* means justice. Perhaps we can coin the term *agathodicy* from *agathon* meaning good, to describe the problem of maintaining the reality of good in a Darwinian world. The two questions, of God and of good, are closely linked since both theists and atheists, who disagree on the reality of God, generally agree that if God is real, He She, or It is the source of goodness. If God is real how do we explain evil? If God is not real, how do we explain good?

This investigation proceeds with an examination of whether a Darwinian understanding of biological evolution and its application to the genesis of the cosmos, forces an atheist conclusion. Some religious believers agree with the hypothetical connection, "If Darwin is right then God does not exist," and conclude that Darwin therefore must be wrong.[19] Materialists, of course, take the opposite position — "Darwin is right, therefore God does not exist." But I will take up the premise that Darwin is, in principle, correct as to the reality of evolution and his proposed mechanism of evolution and ask whether atheism necessarily follows, The atheist argument has three main premises: First, evolution stands as a sufficient explanation of the present world, and so any appeal to a Creator is superfluous. Second, the randomness, waste, and slow pace of evolution exclude the presence of a purpose that would be the signature of a Creator. Third, and most powerful, the violence, pain and suffering of evolving life are incompatible with belief in a decent, much less an all good, Creator.

The Self-sufficiency of Nature and the Case for Atheism

The first argument, that evolution renders the need for a Creator superfluous, rests on the premise that, in the vastness of time and space, anything that could happen will happen somewhere at some time. Advocates of this idea depict biological evolution on earth as just one small instance of physical evolution by which the universe takes on the structure of elements and molecules following patterns, we call laws. When writers such as Daniel Dennett speak of "vastness," they do not limit themselves to the 13.7 billion years or so that mark the progress of our universe since the *big bang*. Rather, they posit a vast if not infinite number of alternate universes that may have no spatial temporal or gravitational relationship with our universe. Every universe that could exist probably does exist and we are part of one that happens to have a structure that supports life and consciousness.[20]

Stephen Hawking and Leonard Mlodinow offer an atheist explanation of reality in their 2010 book, *The Grand Design*. The title is ironic, I assume deliberately so, because theists have traditionally argued that design implies an Intelligent Designer. But Hawking and Mlodinow posit a design without the need for a designer. They contend that the laws of physics can create new universes out of nothing. As Hawking and Mlodinow describe the universe producing laws:

> Any set of laws that describes a continuous world such as ours will have a concept of energy, which is a constant quantity, meaning it does not change in time...One requirement any law of nature must satisfy is that it dictates that the energy of an isolated body surrounded by empty space is positive, which means that one has to do work to assemble the body.[21]

It is not clear whether these laws and concepts, which dictate what energy must do, are aspect of reality or "merely" the brain products of very intelligent physicists, at this stage of human evolution. In the first chapter of *The Grand Design*, the authors stipulate that they are employing a "model dependent realism," which means that our brains must employ a model to interpret the sensory data received by our senses from whatever is real.[22] So there will always be a gap between what even our best physicists know and what really exists.

For Hawking and Mlodinow, and perhaps for all atheistic scientists, the laws constitute an uncaused cause, and given the vastness of time and space, there is no limit to the number of universes that exist, have existed, or will exist. In the view of self-creating universes, each universe may have its own local laws. We are lucky to live in a universe whose laws allow for planets like earth to exist and for life and a degree of intelligence to evolve. But the process that provides for a countless number of universes requires a basic law of energy and gravity that creates from nothing. The nothingness consists of negative energy. Neither atheists nor theists can imagine or think of *nothing,* so we all posit a kind of reality that enables something to come from "nothing."[23] For theists, the reality is a conscious Creator, for atheists the "creative" reality consists of unconscious laws.

Not only do materialists believe that, in a universe such as ours, 13.7 billion years allows for random events to produce life and consciousness, but also that the enormity of time supports the belief that the evolutionary process occurs randomly. The slowness of the process is compatible with randomness, but not with a purposeful Creator. Atheists see the ten billion years from the big bang to the beginning of life on earth, and the 3.5 billion years from the beginning of life to the emergence of human scientists, as a prodigal waste of time. The god in whom atheists do not believe would have been much quicker and more efficient.

Evolution and the Problem of Evil

The argument from evil stands out as the strongest case against belief in God. If an all good and all-powerful Creator produced a world, the argument goes, that world would reflect the Creator's own goodness. But a close look at reality presents something quite different from what we would expect. Life on earth has an inescapable element of violence and can be terrifying and excruciatingly painful at times for its inhabitants. Except for those at the top of the food chain, animals must seek food for themselves and their young live under the constant threat of being eaten by a predator. Their lives are likely to end with a few minutes of terror as they try to escape and then the horror and physical pain of having the claws and teeth of death tear into their flesh.

Psychologist Ernest Becker, writing about how our fear of death, which we try to suppress, describes an absurd nature in which the horror of human death constitutes a small but typical part:

> What are we to make of a creation in which the routine activity is for organisms to tear others apart with teeth of all types––biting, grinding flesh...bones between molars, pushing the pulp greedily down the gullet with delight, incorporating the essence into one's own organization, and then excreting with foul stench and gasses the residue? [24]

Becker argues that if we could remove all the illusions that constitute our culture and look at life as it is, we would realize that nature mocks the poet. In the context of this book, we might conclude that nature mocks the idea of the good.

Why did the Creator not make us all vegetarians like the animals in the "Peaceable Kingdom?" Since plants lack the awareness and the nervous system to feel pain, eating them would not involve inflicting cruelty. Or better, yet, why not endow all creatures with the power of photosynthesis and skip eating all together? But since eating constitutes such a pleasure, why did the Creator not grow lobster tails on trees so that we could enjoy them without throwing a live lobster into boiling water? And why can we not enjoy all sorts of steaks and roasts without the pain and horror of the slaughterhouse? Scientists today are working on growing meat from stem cells. Why didn't an omniscient creator think of that? The contrast between reality and our fantasy of what a benign all-mighty being would have created constitutes for many an airtight argument against belief in God. Atheists like Dawkins do not posit an evil god, but simply an absence of any creator or source of good and evil. The universe including the process of evolution is, in their view is unconscious and pitiless. Atheists have a strong case to show that the world including living things does not flow from an intelligent designer. What happens to the idea of the good?

Creation and Chaos

The notion of God as a designer who controls every event in creation rules out the notion of evolution by natural selection; conversely the acceptance of evolution by natural selection rules out the possibility of belief in God the designer. Religious thinkers who welcome the findings of evolution understand God differently from the theists and the atheists who think of God as a Designer. Theologian John Haught, for example, contends that the discoveries of Darwin open up the possibility of a richer notion of God than had ever been know before. Religious experience, specifically that of Christianity, does not portray God as an all-controlling designer, but as one who empties Himself to allow the world to be itself. As Haught sees it:

> God's creative love constitutes the world as something ontologically distinct from God, and not as a simple extension of divine being. Consequently, the indeterminate natural occurrences that recent physics has uncovered at the

most elementary levels of physical reality, the random events that biology finds at the level of life's evolution, and the freedom that emerges with human existence are all features proper to any world that is permitted and even encouraged to be distinct from the creative love that underlies it.[25]

In Christian belief and experience, God reveals Himself in the form of a poor man, of no political or economic consequence, who suffered death by execution on a cross. The trust in an incomprehensible God, in spite of unbearable sorrow also runs deep in the history of religious Jews, from their early days of exile up through the Holocaust. This notion, of course, has no appeal to those who do not accept it, but it shows that God, as experienced in Christianity and Judaism, bears no resemblance to the powerful but prissy god whom anti-evolutionists affirm, and atheists reject. God as experienced by religion is quite compatible with evolution, for which a variety of mechanisms have been proposed. We can even view it as compatible with Natural Selection. As expressed by the renowned Jesuit paleontologist, Teilhard de Chardin: "Even in the view of a mere biologist, the human epic resembles nothing so much as a way of the cross." [26]

The key issue, as John Haught argues, is not whether the universe is the work of an Intelligent Designer, but whether the universe has purpose. The two questions are different although both sides often run them together as, "The world is either the product of Intelligent Design or it is pointless." Advocates of Intelligent Design, invoke the complexity and beauty of design while atheists claim that the design is sporadic and explainable by randomness over vast periods. Haught's rejection of design is similar to the argument of the atheists in that he contends that evolution does not look like the work of a designer. But Haught, rather than looking back for an original design, looks ahead to an evolving purpose. He further argues that the religions that sprang from Abraham consist primarily in hope for the future.

The question of purposefulness in the universe cannot be answered by science. Scientists can and do express opinions on the issues of purpose, but in doing so they base their judgments on whatever factors cause a person to accept or reject faith in a purposeful universe. Haught compares the fatalism of some scientists to that of the Greek tragedies.[27] Fate for the scientists as for the tragedians moves on with remorseless indifference to human aspirations and comes to a bad conclusion. Shakespeare's Macbeth expressed this powerfully on hearing of his wife's death:

> Life's but a brief shadow; a poor player
> That struts and frets his hour upon the stage
> And then is heard no more: it is a tale
> Told by an idiot, full of sound and fury
> Signifying nothing. [28]

Of course, the scientists who think of the universe as pointless may or may not feel their own life as tragic; they might be quite content with their "hour upon the stage." But regardless of how scientists view life, their view is not part of their science. As Haught argues, science is not equipped to find the value of things. Such questions are metaphysical, and although metaphysics must be consistent with science, a metaphysics of promise is not less scientific than a metaphysics of despair.

John Haught fully embraces the insights of science and especially those of Darwinian evolution. He contends that these scientific insights are not only compatible with the experience of biblical faith, but that they nourish a theology that is richer than pre-Darwinian religious thought. Scientists begin with the commitment to the belief that the world is to some extent intelligible, and that truth is worth the hard work of science. These faith commitments do not prove anything about the ultimate nature of reality, but they are more compatible with a religious vision than with a materialistic one. Unlike the materialist interpretation of reality, the religious view sees the work of the scientist as part of a larger cosmic narrative characterized by a hopeful outcome.[29]

Haught shows the weakness of naïve theism as well as naïve atheism, both of which find a world that grows from random events, as depicted by Darwin, incompatible with belief in God. These theists therefore argue that the events happen by design and the randomness is illusory; the atheists affirm the randomness and declare belief in a Creator to be the illusion. Haught grounds his view of creation in the religious insight that God's love is self-emptying, which allows creation to develop on its own as something other than the Creator. As Haught writes:

> An unrestrained display of infinite presence or "omnipotence" would leave no room for anything other than God, and so it would leave out any evolutionary *self-transcendence* on the part of the cosmos. It is a humble "retreat" on God's part that allows the cosmos to stand on its own and then to evolve as a relatively autonomous reality distinct from its creative ground. In this sense, creation and its evolutionary unfolding would be less the consequence of an eternal divine "plan" than of a humble and loving "letting be." [30]

The crucial meaning of Haught's insights shows that a slowly evolving and chaotic universe does not necessarily lead to a materialist view of reality. Theists and atheist alike cannot get by with a simple choice of affirming or denying design.

Haught's process theology takes a different approach to the notion of God as designer. He maintains that the universe is allowed to grow as something independent of the Creator. He contrasts the understanding of God in process theology with the portrayal of god in naive theism and atheism:

> A coercive deity––one that immature religiosity often wishes for and that our scientific skeptics invariably have in mind when they assert that Darwin has destroyed theism––would not allow for the otherness, autonomy, and self-coherence necessary for a world to be a world unto itself.[31]

A non-coercive creator allows not only human freedom but also the pre-human spontaneity that allows for the formation of the universe and the evolution of life and of species. Haught concludes that God is the source not only of order but also the instability and disorder that are necessary for novelty and for life itself.[32]

While John Haught approaches the issue of evolution as a theologian with a deep understanding of science, Kenneth R. Miller approaches the same question as a cell biologist with a rich understanding of theology. In his book, *Searching for Darwin's God*, Miller begins by demolishing the array of Creationists theories including Intelligent Design. These theories, while claiming the label of "scientific," deny the validity of much well-established science, and they present a diminished notion of God.[33] In chapters 3, 4 and 5, Miller shows that Creationists present God as: first, a charlatan who created the earth only ten thousand years ago, but through fakery, made it look older; second, as a magician who made living things appear out of thin air; and third, as a mechanic who tinkered together the intricacy of the living cell. Miller then demonstrates that the origin of life as well as of species can be accounted for by the scientific study based on Darwinian natural selection.[34]

The conflict that still endures between some religious thinkers and some scientists

stems partly from the notion that religion can answer questions better left to science, for example, questions on the origin of life and origin of species. But the controversy is fueled by many evolutionists who contend that evolution makes mechanistic materialism triumphant to the point that any religious or spiritual ideas are superfluous and irrational.[35] Those evolutionists hold in common with the creationists the premise that evolution and religion are mutually exclusive.

Is Free Will an Illusion?

For centuries, before the ascendancy of physical science, theologians struggled with the question of predestination and free will. If God knows everything that will ever happen, in fact if God causes everything that will ever happen, how can humans be free? If God knows that you are or are not saved, there is nothing you can do about it. With the development of modern physics from the seventeenth to the nineteenth century, physical determinism replaced divine predestination as the cause of all things. Many believers saw God as a cosmic mechanic who set up the laws of the universe, started it running, and then had nothing else to do. In this view, we humans never had anything to do either, since every event, including those in our brain, has a physical cause, and free will is an illusion.[36]

In the twentieth century, the development of quantum physics and the uncertainty principle changed the way we look at the physical universe. Chance events take place at the sub-atomic level so that the physical world is not absolutely determined. These events can affect DNA causing the chance variations that are essential to the notion of biological evolution. The idea of indeterminacy turns the world of physics as well as the world of theology upside-down, since neither the laws of strict determinism nor the mind of God controls all that has happened or will happen. Indeterminacy neither proves nor disproves the reality of God. But it allows that, if God is real, God can intervene in the events of evolution. Similarly, indeterminacy does not prove or disprove human free will, but it allows that there could be a conscious agency that intervenes in the events of our own brains.[37] Unlike the closed view of strict mechanistic determinism that prevailed up to the end of the nineteenth century, the contemporary view of uncertainty allows for the possibility of spiritual agency in the physical universe.

Miller states, as Haught did, that science cannot reveal whether God is real and whether there is purpose in the universe. He contends that much of the atheism and materialism associated with science results from some scientists projecting their personal view on their science and hence on the universe. Miller sees the universe, as revealed by science, to be perfectly compatible with belief in God, and that there is no need for gaps to be filled by magic and miracles. The world is incomplete in the sense that it is still developing, but it is logically complete in structure, especially as revealed by Darwinian evolution. Miller interprets the statement in Genesis, that God created humans according to God's own image and likeness, to mean that our mind is fit to study science and to progress in comprehending the structure of the universe.

While Miller and Haught see contemporary science as liberating us from a mechanistic view of nature, American philosopher William James had struggled with the notion of free will when mechanistic determinism enjoyed supremacy among scientists before the advent of quantum physics. The problem took on a further complication in James's time because most of the thinkers who rejected materialism posited a notion of God as the "Absolute." This notion included the idea that God is all-knowing and all powerful and therefore controlled everything in the universe, past, present, and future. James recognized that this notion of reality left no more room for human agency than did the materialistic notion. In an argument that bears on the notion of the Absolute, as well as whole religious argument against evolution, James observed that God, as experienced in religion bears little resemblance to the notion of a designer who controls every aspect of creation and guarantees a neat outcome.

James describes reality as a battleground on which our salvation is possible but not guaranteed. Facing the evil of the world, we may succumb to the nightmarish view, or even the suicidal view, that *our* world is evil beyond hope. But if we take up the challenge and believe in a hopeful outcome, we make the hopeful possibility become a reality. James proposed belief in a God who could take strength from our little efforts. Although the influence of anyone of us is small, together we are integral to any outcome of the world. A world that involves danger and struggle fits our nature better than a world with no hope and even better than a world with no risk. As James sums up his view:

> If this life be not a real fight, in which something is eternally gained for the universe by success, it is no better than a game of theatricals from which one may withdraw at will. But it *feels like a real fight*--as if there were something really wild in the universe which we, with all our idealities and faithfulness, are needed to redeem; but first to redeem our own hearts from atheisms and fears. [38]

For James, the notion of God and humans struggling together to create and redeem a world is more compatible with religion and with human nature than either a hopeless materialism or belief in a smug God who creates effortlessly while we look on as spectators.

Although James's account of God would not be satisfactory to most classical theologians, it would fit the view of some process theologians.[39] More importantly, whatever value James's idea has for theology, he does show that a chaotic world, in which suffering, risk, and loss are real, is compatible with historical religion.

The above arguments intend to show that, contrary to naïve theists and atheists, belief in God is compatible with a Darwinian world-view with it slowness and with the intermingling of good and evil. Biblical religion does not portray God as a designer who makes the world easily out of his own substance. Rather, God can be hoped for as a Creator drawing the world out of nothingness, through all-in-division, toward a harmony whose fulfillment is up ahead. Scientists can continue to explore the world and bring it into ever more general laws, whether the scientists believe that all reality is a random arrangement of things in the vastness of time and space, or whether they believe that there is a rational purpose leading the way. While the former view would seem to call for a philosophy of the absurd, the latter view is more hospitable to the project of science. James contended that theism is a more rational view than any of its opponents. Of course, we cannot assume, without circular argument, that the more rational view is true.

The first chapter outlined the opposition between a spiritual worldview in which consciousness precedes nature, and the materialist view in which consciousness is a small and relatively insignificant product of matter. For the spiritual view, evil presents a major problem, which Chapter 2 wrestled with. For the materialist view, evil does not constitute a metaphysical problem, but merely consists in our subjective discontent with the way things are. The spiritual view assumes the primacy of what we call "the good." The materialist view sees the good as our subjective approval of some situations. The next chapter will explore the idea of good.

Chapter 3:
The Goodness of Nature and the Shroud of Evil

Traditional Notion of Good

The pre-Darwin worldview allowed for a less problematic understanding of the relation between *being* and *good*. We can think of Plato's notion that The Good is beyond being, but serves as the source of all other being. In Plato's analogy the Good is to the world of ideal forms, what the sun is to visible reality. Just as the sun serves as the cause of the material world and makes it visible,[40] the Good causes the forms and makes them knowable. The forms are more real and more perfect than the visible objects that constitute inferior copies or images of the forms. Compared to visible things the forms are more real and share more perfectly in the ultimate form, the Good. That which is bad is less real than that which is good.[41] In presenting a traditional understanding of the goodness of reality, I am not trying to make a case for it. Rather, I am trying to set it in front of us so that it can become a basis for comparison.

Aristotle defined the good as that at which all things aim, and all things aim at the fulfillment of their nature.[42] Something is bad if it lacks a quality that belongs to the fulfillment of its purpose. You cannot have a good race horse that lacks speed, or a good workhorse that lacks strength. To use human examples, a good quarterback cannot lack arm strength, and a good surgeon cannot lack manual dexterity. In all of these cases, we are not talking about moral good and evil, of course, but about qualities that enable an animal or a human to achieve its intended purpose.

The relation between purpose and good, which is found in all of nature and in non-moral qualities in humans, is also found at the level of human morality. Aristotle defines a human as a rational animal, and a person is one who has actualized the human potential for rationality. Good moral qualities constitute virtues which consist of habits of living according to reason, and in most cases involve avoiding the extremes of excess and deficiency. For example, the virtue of temperance in eating means that a person eats the right amount of food relative to the needs of the individual person rather than eating too much or too little. Courage consists of the quality that enables a person to face danger when reasonable and avoid both cowardliness and rashness. A bad person fails to actualize the ability to live reasonably, which means virtuously. Living reasonably is the defining characteristic of a human being. Unlike the virtuous persons, morally under-developed persons would not control their own passion and desire or learn to live justly in society. Goodness, for us, means actualizing our nature as human beings. Since being is good, we become better by actualizing our potential for the kind of being that we are. In this worldview, moral evil, like all evil, is a *lack,* a failure to become a fully actualized being.

The affirmation of the goodness of being finds one of its fullest expressions in the metaphysics of St. Thomas Aquinas. Being and good are coextensive; whatever *is*, is good. The *concepts* of being and good are distinct in that the idea of good adds something to the idea of being, namely, the relationship to a will. St. Thomas called the relationship between reality and God's will *essential.* Since he believed that God is the creative source of all that is, everything that is created is good because God loves it. For us humans, the relationship between being and our will is not essential. In our case, we can love all reality because it is good.

But as Chapter Two pointed out, and as our lived life screams at us, the world does not look like the product of a Creator who made all things good. The problem of evil asserts itself in every discussion of the good. For St. Thomas, if all being is good, evil must be non-being, a lack of something that ought to be. We can think of physical evils such as blindness, although we ordinarily do not use the term evil, but rather misfortune. For us to lose our eyesight is a misfortune because sight is a normal part of a human being's experience. We love our eyesight and see it as a good. A premature death is a misfortune because we view life as good. All the bad things that happen to us from the loss of property in a fire or flood, to the loss of a relationship, are bad precisely because that which is lost is good. *The evil consists of the lack of something that we deeply wish to be there.* Moral evil, as stated above in the discussion of Aristotle and virtue, is the lack of a quality that ought to be part of a human being's character.

The Thomistic view, that being and good are coextensive, includes the affirmation that being and truth are also coextensive. Just as "good" adds relationship to a will to the concept of "being," so "truth" adds relationship to a mind. The world is understood as rational and "legible" because it flows from the mind of God.[43] This is not a "creationist" idea in the sense of biblical literalism. Although St. Thomas lived six centuries too early to know about evolution, his understanding of creation is compatible with evolution. Of course it is not compatible with a materialistic interpretation of evolution. The principle idea of God's creative mind and will does not refer only to the beginning, whether the beginning is a very busy week in 4004 BC, or the Big Bang of 13. 7 billion years ago.

The essential notion of God as a Creator means that in spite of all the disorder, there is an underlying order that makes the scientific study of evolution, as well as evolution itself possible.

The problems for anyone who sees creation as the work of rationality and love is challenged today more that they would have been in the thirteenth century. The universe as we know it is almost infinitely vaster than anything that could have been imagined in the days before Galileo. The enormity of chaos, violence and irrationality is also almost infinitely greater.

The Problem of Good in the Modern Age

The world revealed to us by contemporary science does not resemble the ordered world of Aristotle in the Golden Age of Greek culture and learning, nor the world of St. Thomas in the flowering of medieval learning in the 13th century. It doesn't even resemble the Newtonian view that inspired the Enlightenment when Alexander Pope wrote, "And God said 'Let Newton be' and all was light." The happy age of light was thrown back into darkness by the grim details of Darwinian evolution and into confusion by the discovery of quantum physics and relativity. The violent and unhappy state of affairs that we humans subjectively judge as evil seems to be simply the way things are. Affirming the reality of "good," much less an all-good Creator, becomes more and more problematic. Quoting Alexander Pope again, the more apt metaphor for reality might be:

Thy hand, Great Chaos, lets the curtain fall
And universal darkness covers all.

The key question consists of whether the pervasiveness of darkness, both physical and metaphorical, precludes the possibility of a powerful and good Creator. Two easy, but perhaps feasible, solutions would be to deny the darkness or to deny the Creator. The first solution deals with the problem of evil by making evil an illusion or a subjective human attitude. The second solution does the same with the problem of good.

Here I will follow the lead of those who acknowledge the reality of brute facts in the formation of the universe, and especially of the brutal dimension in the evolution of life on earth, and yet maintain a rational belief in a Creator God and the reality of the good.

I will briefly address an argument from theodicy used by some theists to explain evil.[44] Without necessarily affirming a literal interpretation of Genesis or denying evolution, they affirm the theological tenant that God created the world good, but that evil resulted from free will. To express this idea in popular terms, God could have kept the world good, as God intended it to be. But in order to have a creature who could love God freely, we were endowed with free will. It is the misuse of free will that brought evil into the world.

I maintain that we should stop blaming free will for evil. The most obvious reason for asserting that this explanation falls far short is that it does not address the chaos, suffering, and horror that abound in nature apart from any human agency. But it even fails to explain human moral evil. If free will were the cause of all evil, we could expect that the "default" mode of every human being would be good, and that evil acts would require an act of will. But as William James had pointed out, free will takes effort, whereas following our impulses does not. James argues that "attention with effort" constitutes the essential meaning of an act of free will. "*The essential achievement of the will, in short, when it is most 'voluntary' is to* ATTEND *to a difficult object and hold it fast before our mind* (emphasis in the original).[45] Without free will, or if we fail to develop our ability to attend to difficult ideas so that they may govern our actions, we sink into evil behavior. It does not take a firm resolution or any special discipline to be greedy, lustful, lazy, or envious. By contrast, it takes a life-time of training to develop our free will and to become virtuous.[46] So free will stands as one of the good things that we need to take account of rather than an explanation of evil.

After this brief side trip on free will, the argument returns to the question of how we can acknowledge the reality of evil and yet believe in a Creator God and the reality the good. One thinker who leads the way on this line of thinking is theologian John Haught, who was cited in Chapter 2. Haught supports the notion of God who is not a designer. If we think of God by analogy to a human designer, say of landscapes, cars, or clothing, we think of one who makes a careful plan before working it out in the material world. But as Haught points out, the history of the universe, especially the evolution of life reveals novelty and surprises. As a theologian, he advises us to look for God, not in some primal past as a designer, but rather, in his phrase, "up ahead" in the novelty and surprises that evolution has to offer. He contends that to be a Creator, God must not only create order, but must also create chaos. A design would be a fixed plan, but from chaos new realties can be born. Consistent with this idea, we find evolution, from the start of life to the advent of humans, as continuously surprising us with increases of consciousness, events that are happening with an accelerating tempo. [47]

Chaos as the Default Mode

Building on Haught's insights, I offer a variation on the theme of creation and chaos by affirming that if there is a God-Creator. God does not need to create chaos; chaos is the default mode that exhibits lack of creation. If God is a perfect being, all-in-harmony, then nothingness is all-in-division, complete chaos and disorder. My description rests on the assumption that "nothingness" remains unthinkable. But if we can *imagine* nothingness and creation *ex nihilo*, the first stage of creation would be all-in-division. The process of world-formation would consist first of drawing the most elemental particles into more harmonious configurations such as atoms, then molecules. Once life begins, the story becomes much more interesting, at least for us living creatures on earth.

Atheists, as described in Chapter Two, see the 10 billion or so years from the *big bang* to the beginning of life on earth, and the 3.8 billion years from the beginning of life to emergence of human scientists, as a prodigal waste of time, and evidence that there is no creative intelligence at work. But during this time the heavy elements such as carbon formed in stars and exploded and scattered throughout the universe. These explosions produced the earth with all the right stuff to allow life to begin.

In both physical and biological evolution, two factors oppose each other. The opposing forces include the tendency toward cooperation that accounts for molecules, then cells, ultimately organisms working together to sustain life. But countering the move toward cooperation we find the competitive tendency to see the other as an enemy to be avoided or destroyed. On the level of inert matter, the elements appear to be impenetrable and repel each other. But they also form bonds and become parts of more complex atoms and molecules. At the level of life on earth, organisms fight to the death for survival, but also form symbiotic communities and develop in complexity. In biological evolution two factors oppose each other. We can see this dual tendency from the most fundamental particles up to and including human society. Inert matter is impenetrable; organisms fight to the death for survival. The conflict takes place between the original nothingness, the all-in-division, from which beings are called and the harmony to which they are called. The tragic irony consist in the fact that the more reality and integration that an entity has, the more destructive it can be in its pursuit of self-preservation. So the process from non-being to being exhibits the best and the worst.

In the preceding paragraphs, I used some problematic phrases such as "drawing the most elemental particles into more harmonious configurations," "the harmony to which (beings) are called," and "pursuit of self-preservation." These expressions constitute anthropomorphic metaphors, and as I pointed out above, materialists also use such metaphors. As Hawking and Mlodinow say of their own work, it makes use of "model-dependent realism." Whatever view we have of reality, it must be filtered and formulated by human understanding and language. The "inner" working of non-sentient entities remains hidden from us. Even within our conscious life we do not understand the movement of the impulses on which our consciousness depends––for example, the impulse that travels from our conscious choice to type a word to the movement of our fingers on the keyboard. Physiologists can explain the movements from the brain to the fingers, but only from the "outside."

Randomness occurs in the firing of neurons in our brain and nervous system but unless we suffer from a debilitating disease, we are able to harness the neuron-firing enough to move meaningfully through life. A materialist might counter that the consciousness is a mere by-product of the neuro-physiological events rather than a power that causes or even directs the impulses. Some refer to consciousness as an "epi-phenomenon" meaning that, in Bertrand Russell's analogy, consciousness can no more move the nerves than the smoke from the chimney of a locomotive can move the train. The only advantage that this theory has going for it is its ability to maintain the materialist world-view. But even Leonard Mlodinow, in a book emphasizing the predominance of randomness in determining the outcome of whatever happens in life, affirms the ability to put forth effort.[48]

Randomness and Law

When scientists look at elements from the outside, they can discern both randomness and law. Without randomness there would be no change and therefore no evolution. Without lawfulness, there would be no preservation of change and therefore no science, and no scientists or other living things. The contrast and sometimes conflict between randomness and lawfulness does not constitute a dualism between nature and spirit.

A very brief historical synopsis of dualism can help situate the contrast that I am presenting. A dualism between matter and spirit pervaded much, but not all, of ancient and medieval thought. For example, Plato compared the study of philosophy to dying because its purpose was to free the soul from the distractions and limitations of the body. Although official Christianity rejected the view that matter and spirit were in radical opposition to each other, some forms of Christian asceticism saw the need to subdue the body through fasting, suffering, and deprivation, so that the soul could be free. By contrast, The Enlightenment provided a view of nature as divinely ordered so that Newtonian physics and Jeffersonian democracy were possible.

In the nineteenth century, many social, economic and cultural events undermined the notion of a world that is providentially ordered. The most important event philosophically was probably the publication of Darwin's *Origin of Species* (1859), which not only led many thinkers to the notion that there was no need to posit a God-Creator, but that the brutality of the process is incompatible with such a God.

A post-Darwin natural morality emerged with a theme of "survival of the fittest." Herbert Spencer, who coined the term, applied it not only to Darwin's biological natural selection but also to economic and social policy, an idea that came to be known as "Social Darwinism." Industrialist, Andrew Carnegie, expressed his debt to Darwin and Spencer for providing an ethical and philosophical background for his industrialization and the harsh living conditions that accompanied it. Carnegie justified any harm done to people and to the environment by trusting that "All is well since all gets better." The optimistic thinking of the Enlightenment was not abandoned, it was just projected into the future.

Morality and Nature

The social reformers who saw the need to reverse the fortunes of the working class believed that they had to act contrary to the principle of natural selection. They believed that rather than live by the "law of the jungle," our humanity required us to take care of the weak and the poor. Rather than follow a "natural law," morality involves acting in spite of nature, or even against nature.

Two examples, one from the late 19th century and the other from the late 20th century illustrate the divorce of morality from nature in the wake of Darwin. The first is William James, who referring not to a natural morality, but to a natural spirituality, said that such a thing is impossible. The romantic view of nature that flourished in the 18th century is built on an illusion. In his lecture, "Is Life Worth Living," he emphasized the role of religion in an affirmative answer to the title question. But he agreed with those who held that "the physical order of nature, taken simply as science knows it, cannot be held to reveal any one harmonious spiritual intent. It is mere *weather*...doing and undoing without end." [49] James, whose background was scientific biology and psychology, asserted that "Our science is a drop, our ignorance a sea." [50] As an interesting aside, James loved nature, and hiking and camping were among his favorite activities.

Morality requires some degree of spirituality since free will cannot exist without some independence of the mind from the brain. In James's one essay on moral theory, "The Moral Philosopher and the Moral Life," he explicitly rejects the notion that we can find the good in the nature of things. Rather, the good is simply what conscious beings, human or divine, claim to be good. Therefore, the highest good is to create a moral universe, or as he calls it, a moral republic, in which as many claims as possible can be satisfied. In James's pluralistic view, we may try to connect as many things as possible, but some things will remain unconnected. When the material world perishes, as it ultimately must, we may hope for salvation in a non-material realm.

The second example of divorcing morality from nature is Richard Dawkins, an uncompromising atheist and materialist, who nevertheless holds that we can create morality by opposing nature. In his 1976 book, *The Selfish Gene,* he argues that all living things are disposed to preserve, not their own individual life, but the genes that they carry. In the process of natural selection, the only genes that survive in the long run are those that direct their hosts to replicate themselves. So if parents, of any species, sacrifice themselves for the sake of their offspring, their genes will survive. The genes of parents, or potential parents who do not care about their offspring, will die with the individual organisms. So every organism that has survived so far has a strong inclination to pass on its genes. But human beings alone have the ability to act contrary to the "selfish gene." As was stated in Chapter 1, we may act contrary to the natural inclination to preserve our genes out of either individual selfishness, or out of an altruistic care for those who are not in our genetic line. Much moral thinking after Darwin holds that if the good exists at all, we can find it or create it only apart from nature or contrary to nature.

A Contemporary Defense of the Good

John Haught, however, argues for a morality rooted in nature. Haught argues that in order to connect our moral life to the natural world, we would have to "...discern in the cosmic process some general aim or purposiveness with which our own life might be morally aligned." [51] In ancient and medieval worldviews of Aristotle and St Thomas, the connection between nature and ethics appeared to be obvious. Every natural creature as well as every human ethical act could be understood in terms of seeking an end or fulfillment. But Haught contends that, in spite of the apparent chasm between nature and human ethical striving, we can develop a metaphysics that is compatible with science, and that presents the cosmos with meaningfulness coinciding with human striving. For this purpose he draws on "process theology" that stems from the metaphysics of Alfred North Whitehead. [52]

Haught acknowledges that the ruthlessness found in nature seems to exclude the possibility of some overarching purpose in the universe. He mentions that most theologians attempted to find meaning in human experience in spite of the meaninglessness of the non-human natural world. But Haught credits Whitehead for developing a cosmology that unites our human striving with the whole history of the universe. Haught contends that Whitehead's philosophy and the process theology that flowed from it perceives the universe as a process in which all the contrasting and conflicting occasions merge into a harmony of contrasts that expresses an intense cosmic beauty.

The shaping of the universe expresses an "aesthetic cosmological principle" by which the elements are being brought into harmony. This idea is different from what some have called the "anthropic cosmological principle," which sees the whole universe as leading toward the emergence of the human race. The aesthetic principle sees the whole process as leading to the production of beauty, of which the emergence of humanity constitutes an aspect. As Haught phrases it, the emergent beauty that stands out in our terrestrial experience is "...the emergence of life, subjectivity, freedom, consciousness, and community.[53] As the universe grows in complexity, it most probably grows in consciousness, not only on earth, but throughout the universe. The correspondence of complexity and consciousness will be taken up in the chapter on consciousness.

In this chapter I tried to show how good can be seen beneath the seemingly overwhelming evil in the physical world. The next point that I want to develop is that good consists in the fulfillment of what John

Haught called the aesthetic principle. Consciousness slowly becomes embodied in nature. The process often happens all too slowly in terms of a human life span, but it is happening. This embodiment of consciousness presents itself to us most obviously in the physical and cultural evolution of the human species. But it can also be readily seen when we consider a broad orderly but non-linear view of the development of consciousness in which we see its emergence in relative pulses from the beginning of life on earth to the emergence of humans.[54] The next chapter will present the emergence of the Good in the evolution of consciousness and freedom.

Chapter 4:
Consciousness, Freedom, and Evolution

The subject of consciousness would overflow even a very large tome devoted to describing it. The purpose of this chapter must be limited to demonstrating consciousness as the exemplar of good in the universe. Part of the task consists in showing how consciousness develops in evolving species like our own, and how freedom flows from consciousness.

My reasoning about consciousness in the context of "the problem of the good" rests on the assumption that the growth and development of consciousness stands out as a commonly accepted instance of something which is good. Anyone reading this paragraph will probably agree, or they would not be reading this or anything else. While it is true that a person suffering clinical depression might prefer sleep to wakefulness, wish they had not been born, and become suicidal, they and anyone who loves them, would clearly see their state as a tragic misfortune. Much of psychotherapy consists of enabling people to enjoy greater consciousness. The same can be said of most medical care and of almost all education.

Do We Know What Consciousness Is?

A nearly insurmountable problem faces us at the beginning of any conversation about consciousness, namely, trying to state clearly the very nature of consciousness. For starters, it is indefinable. Consciousness stands alone as a reality that does not belong to any genus and is not like anything else. We can approach the subject of consciousness as theologians approach a discussion of God—by using the twofold approach of first, what they call the *via negativa,* and second, analogy. The first method, the *via negative,* shows what consciousness is *not.* The second method, analogy, shows what consciousness is like. Further, we can look at conscious development both in the individual and in the species to show how consciousness moves from mere sensation, to perception, judgment, reasoning, and beyond. A problem presents itself in that all of these methods assume that we already know what consciousness is. The good news is that in fact we do know what consciousness is. Everyone who has ever thought of this question already knows what consciousness is. So the only task of this work is to articulate and interpret consciousness to show how it exemplifies the problem of the good.

Although we cannot define consciousness, we can *describe* it in the literal sense of the word "describe," meaning that we can write about it. We can also talk about it and certainly think about it. We come to understand consciousness by contrast to unconsciousness as when we temporarily lose consciousness because of an accident or anesthesia. Other contrasts include sleeping and wakefulness, dreaming and awareness of our external surroundings, and boredom compared to full interest.

We can further clarify our understanding of consciousness by comparing the poles of a spectrum from material to spiritual. If there is a totally non-conscious being, what is it like? Imagine a particle of matter as conceived in traditional Newtonian science. It appears to be dead, inert, moved and determined only by external forces, and impenetrable. By contrast, whether or not we believe that any non-material being exists, we can *think* of a pure spirit, in contrast to matter, as conscious, self-determined, and able to enter communion with other spiritual beings. We humans are obviously not pure spirits and we have much of Newtonian inertness about us. But if we have a degree of self-awareness, self-determination, and openness to community, then we are to that extent spiritual. An increase in spirituality as I use the term here, coincides with an increase in consciousness.

When we have moments of heightened awareness, we experience a more clear and intense knowledge of our world, a greater sense of freedom, and a feeling of oneness with people and perhaps things around us. Such heightened states may be generated from a wide and diverse range of human activity as reported by those who experience life-threatening emergencies, or from sports, music, contemplation of nature, and traditional religious meditation. We can imagine that consciousness, freedom, and communion extend to infinity as all of our ordinary physical and psychological limitations lose their hold. Every spiritual tradition claims saints and mystics who actually experience unity with infinite being.[55]

When in Doubt, Start with William James

The vastness of literature on consciousness presents a problem of selection, especially for selecting a starting point. In this case, I will follow a personal maxim: "When in doubt, start with William James." In his *Principles of Psychology* (1890), James writes extensively about the meaning of consciousness. He points out that no one can deny that they have "states of consciousness," although finding an adequate vocabulary to describe them poses enormous problems.[56] Everyone who thinks about thought, including those in what was then the new science of psychology, can distinguish between the object of the thought and the thought itself. If they turn to reflective introspection, thinking about the thought itself, they can distinguish between the thought and the thinker. The thought is part of what James calls the empirical self, the "me." But the thinker is the "I." When I try to think of the thinker, I make it an object, part of the empirical me. While I cannot deny that there is a subjective thinker, its nature eludes me. For the sake of creating a naturalistic psychology, James defers the metaphysical question of what the thinker is, and limits himself to describing the most recent thought as the thinker. If I introspectively try to capture this thought, it is now a part of the empirical me, which consists of all the thoughts of which I am aware. A new thought is now making this judgment.

In his later works, James takes on the metaphysical question of consciousness. The "Conclusions" to his 1909 work, *A Pluralistic Universe*, describes "religious experiences of a specific nature." [57] Significantly, James calls them "experiences," rather than objects of faith or reason. These experiences reveal a range of happiness and power that supersedes our naturalistic thinking and "seem to show a world that is wider than either physics or philistine ethics can imagine." He describes these experiences as a kind of life after death. Here, James does not mean our biological death, but rather, "...death of hope, death of strength...death of everything that paganism, naturalism, and legalism pin their faith on and tie their trust to."[58] James contends that reasoning would never have inferred these experiences of a larger world revealing itself after the experience of despair. But once they reveal themselves, anyone trying to develop a more complete philosophy must take them into account.

These experiences give individuals a sense that their own consciousness is continuous with a wider self from which the experience flows in. Describing an individual life as being "continuous with a *more* of the same quality, which is operative in the universe outside of him," James refers to "words which I have used elsewhere," an allusion to the "Conclusions" of his 1901 Gifford Lectures, *The Varieties of Religious Experience.* [59] In this work, James provides more insights on consciousness than this chapter can accommodate. The experiences he describes in terms of expanded consciousness include unifying the divided soul, conversion, saintliness, and mysticism. In his chapter "Mysticism," he expresses what he calls a truth that had earlier forced itself on his mind:

> It is that our normal waking consciousness, rational consciousness as we call it, is but one special type of consciousness, whilst all about it, parted from it by the filmiest of screens, there lie potential forms of consciousness entirely different? [60]

Throughout the *Varieties,* James offers experiential evidence that consciousness consists of much more than the awareness of any single human organism.

In the "Conclusions" he offers a way to interpret the larger consciousness. These experiences; conversion, saintliness, and mysticism, reveal a larger world from which our ordinary consciousness draws its significance. On the near side, it seems to be an extension of the conscious individual self. But it may extend further to include what religious believers call God. Based on the real impact that the larger consciousness has on human lives, often leading to heroic work and saintly behavior toward others, James infers that what seems to be a higher consciousness is in fact higher and greater than the individual, rather than something that the individual brain secretes.

If James's interpretation holds true, then consciousness is prior to matter, specifically prior to the matter of any individual brain. As the brain develops in human evolution and in the maturing of the individual, it becomes a vessel of what we call consciousness. In this interpretation, growth in consciousness, manifested in greater awareness, intelligence, and love, stands out as the goal of human life. From this point of view, whatever promotes the development of consciousness is good; whatever inhibits it is evil.

A Reductionist View of Consciousness

The whole notion of consciousness as a reality independent of and higher than the brain has come under attack in recent years. Scientists and philosophers, most notably Daniel Dennett and Francis Crick have presented explanations reducing consciousness to brain molecules. As noted in Chapter One, Francis Crick in his 1994 book, *the Astonishing Hypothesis,* depicted consciousness and the very awareness of self as nothing but the activity of molecules. Daniel Dennett offered extended arguments for understanding both consciousness and freedom in physical terms In *Consciousness Explained* (1991), and *Freedom Evolves* (2003).

Christof Koch, a younger colleague of Francis Crick took on the project of fully explaining consciousness in physical reductionist terms. In his 2012 book, *Consciousness: Confessions of a Romantic Reductionist,* Koch sets out to "describe a plausible quantitative theory of consciousness that explains why certain types of highly organized matter, in particular brains, can be conscious."[61] Koch argues that consciousness will ultimately be explained by the physical sciences, especially neuro-biology. But while he insists that consciousness cannot exist without matter, he rejects the notion that the reduction of consciousness to the activity of billions of tiny nerve cells excludes the possibility of meaning in the universe. [62]

Koch grapples with *the hard problem,* a term used by David Chalmers, which refers to understanding why anybody can be conscious at all. He summarizes the great progress that neuroscience is making in connecting conscious states with neural events, but admits that all the science is from a third person point of view. He poses the question that involves the hard problem from a reductionist's perspective: "...how does nervous tissue acquire an interior first-person point of view?" [63] Koch rejects the notion that the gap between brain's mechanisms and consciousness is unbridgeable, dismissing such views as defeatist and a denigration of reason. His premise asserts that since science has been the best method for understanding the external world, it should also help us explain the interior world of consciousness. [64]

Koch contends that science can close the gap that still separates neurological understanding of the brain and actual first-person states of consciousness. Describing the advances that have been made in exploration of the brain he writes: "Neuroscience textbooks describe this organ in mind-numbing detail yet leave out what it means to be the owner of one." [65] Koch intends to make up for this "remarkable omission" by showing the link between the experiencing subject and the perspective of the brain scientist. His specific goal is to find what he and Francis Crick call the neural correlates of consciousness (NCC) defined as "the minimal neural mechanisms jointly sufficient for any one specific conscious concept." [66]

It would seem that if he is successful, he will have refuted my thesis as explained in Chapter One, namely that it is reasonable to believe that consciousness precedes matter. But even If Koch, or other researchers show how matter becomes conscious by developing a highly complex brain, and I am assuming that they will, it will show what a material being needs to be conscious, but not necessarily entail that all consciousness requires a material base. A full explanation of how matter becomes conscious leaves open the question of whether any conscious reality existed prior to matter becoming conscious.

Centrality of the Question of Free Will

The issue of free will is closely linked to the meaning of consciousness because the whole question of free will asks whether consciousness can determine matter without being completely determined by matter. Put more specifically, can the conscious subject decide on particular brain events without the decision having been predetermined by other brain events? For example, consider a person who resolves to improve his or her fitness by taking up running. It seems, from the person's point of view, that the resolution causes the mind to focus on health and fitness so that physical changes take place. The person now devotes time and energy to running on a road or track, time that would otherwise have been spent on some sedentary activity such as watching television. But was the origin and continuation of the resolution caused by some other physical brain event of which the person had neither awareness nor control? Here I will resume the dialogue with Christof Koch's *Consciousness*.

Koch offers as a definition of free will: "You are free if, under identical circumstances, you could have acted otherwise. Identical circumstances refer to not only the same external conditions but also the same brain states." [67] He considers debates on the reality of free will to be futile since we cannot go back and do things differently. I think that his observation about the futility of debates on free will stems from his definition rather than on the real possibility of free will. His definition looks backward, "Could you have acted differently?"

This definition sets up a sure failure for free will since, to the best of my knowledge, no free will theory would say that we are free to change the past. What's done is done. But free will takes on a different meaning when we apply it to the future. The question of free will can be restated as: "Can I, through 'attention with effort,' make my future different from what it would be without such effort." The phrase, "attention with effort," flows from William James and his notion that ideas control action and that through effort we can determine which ideas control our action. This understanding need not slip into futility since it has a real impact. Suppose a young person heard this idea from someone whom she respects and tries to apply it to her life. Would this notion not make a difference in the way she lived? The practical significance of this question can best be understood by reviewing William James's description of free will.

According to James, every idea has some bodily expression, and ideas either instigate or inhibit muscular movements. Since we generally have several ideas at any one time, some contradicting others, we act on the most dominant one. We are free if and only if we can, by effort, make a chosen idea dominant by deliberately attending to it. For example, a person who has a plate of fried chicken in front of him may eat it without effort since the dominant idea is how good it tastes. But if the same person turns his attention to the desirability of clean arteries and a healthy body weight, he may, through effort, make this healthy image dominant and so change his eating habits. The whole question of free will comes down to whether "we," our conscious selves, can determine the ideas that we attend to and the amount of effort that we can exert to maintain the attention.

If the materialists are right, then the whole process of "attention with effort" originates in molecules of which we may not be consciously aware, and "we" are mere spectators of a process over which we have no control. We cannot prove that the materialists are right or wrong. However, it is reasonable to believe that we can, perhaps to a very small degree, choose what we think is good, pay attention to it with effort, and thereby make our lives different from what they otherwise would be. If this assumption is true, then we have a free will and *consciousness has a degree of control over matter.*

Koch offers two reasons to doubt that consciousness can exert control over matter. The first reason is based on the conservation of energy. Anything that happens in the physical world depends on the existing energy. Nothing happens without using some amount of energy that constitutes the physical universe. So the neural correlates of thought, the physical conditions necessary for any thought, depend on some physical event. They cannot originate from any non-physical entity, even if there are non-physical entities.

Koch leaves an infinitesimal crack in the closed neuro-physical system that may provide an opportunity for free will, but he considers the degree of freedom to be insignificant, and on a practical level, indistinguishable from mere chance. In describing the one opportunity for free will, Koch refers to the view of Karl Popper and John Eccles, advocates of free will, that "the conscious mind imposes its will onto the brain by manipulating the way neurons communicate with each other in the regions of the cortex concerned with the planning of movement." According to the Popper-Eccles view, the mind need not supply the physical energy for the movement of the chemical signals, but it can "direct traffic" by promoting activity in theses neurons and preventing it in those. But Koch argues that such influence is possible only in quantum-mechanical states in which there is a certain probability that a synapse will or will not switch. According to his argument, the mind cannot change the probability, but it might determine what will happen on any given event. Control over a single event does not change the probability that the person will act this way rather than that way. But, we may ask, if the mind can control this one event, might it also influence the next one and the one after? Could this type of influence, over time, not change the probability?

Koch follows up with further arguments against the feasibility of free will.[68] He cites and describes experimental evidence that brain activity that instigates an apparent act of will, actually begins before the actor is aware of making a decision. In Koch's example, a person indicates the instant that he or she decides to move an arm. The actual movement of the arm coincides with the moment of their awareness, but EEG information shows that the process has started prior to the decision. This experiment implies that what we feel is a free choice is, in fact, the result of brain activity of which we are unaware.

However, free will is not about a single action but about a life-time of habit formation. In the case of the arm movement experiment, it might be just as well if unconscious neuro-physical events choose the moment to move an arm. But there are many human activities in which it is crucial to choose a particular act at just the right moment. Such examples abound especially in sports. For example, if a baseball player is deciding to steal second base, he must pick the right moment. If he leaves a second too early, he might get picked off; a second too late and he will be thrown out. So an unconscious physical brain event, which occurs before the actual steal attempt, might serve him better than slower conscious deliberation. But a baseball player has spent a lot of time deliberately developing the habit of running bases. He has chosen to develop these habits, therefore he has chosen the neural pathways that enable him to seize the moment without deliberation. The deliberate development of habits applies to all sports, music, dancing, cooking, hunting, and many other activities. We may freely choose to spend time developing these skills. When time sensitivity is not an issue, we are free to the extent that, over time, we can choose how we develop our habitual behavior. The habits serve us well when we must act "in the blink of an eye." While the above description does not "prove" free will, it does provide a feasible belief in free will that survives Koch's argument against it.

A further look at Koch reveals that he himself believes in free will. He affirms a "compatibilist" notion of free will, which means that you are free if and only if you can follow your own desires and preferences. For example, smokers who wish to stop smoking are free or not free depending on whether they are able to follow their desire to stop. Some can and some can't. But even in the case of those who successfully follow their desire, the desires themselves stem from biological and psychological events over which the person has no authorship.[69] The compatibilist definition entails some implications that even the compatibilists should find problematic. For example, the person who wishes to smoke would be free if he were allowed to smoke without limitations and prohibitions. The same holds true of those who wish to express their preference for unlimited acquisitions, sexual encounters, or physical expressions of anger. In Koch's case, he not only wants to be able to express his desires and preferences without coercion or prohibition, but also specifies what he wants his desires to be. I assume that this is also true of most other materialists in spite of their theory.

It is worth quoting Koch at length to show his position regarding free will.

After rejecting both classical determinism that sees the future as already fixed, and also rejecting the notion that an immaterial "soul" can influence matter, he concludes:

> I've taken two lessons from these insights. First, I've adopted a more pragmatic compatibilist conception of free will. *I strive* to live as free of external and internal constraints as possible. The only exception should be constraints that *I deliberately and consciously impose upon myself,* chief among them, constraints motivated by ethical concerns; whatever you do, do not hurt others and *try* to leave the planet a better place than you found it. Other considerations include family, health, financial stability, and mindfulness. Second, *I try* to understand my unconscious motivations, fears, and desires better. I reflect deeper about my own actions and emotions than my younger self did. (emphases added). [70]

Who or what is the "I" that "strives," "deliberately and consciously imposes," and "tries?" It seems that if consciousness has no autonomy, we can only hope that our molecules will do these things or, depending on the molecules, hope that they don't. A dogmatic materialist may argue that Koch has gone soft in the paragraph quoted above. But, on the contrary, the hopeful resolute paragraph may simply show the limitation of materialism.

Brain States and Subjectivity

Koch's analysis of the relationship between brain states and the subjective feeling of agency has only two possible solutions, one of which he rejects. The apparent options are that either further search will prove an unbridgeable gap between consciousness and physical science, or the progress of neuro-science will explain away the feeling of agency as nothing but the behavior of molecules. Koch considers the first option as the defeat of science.

The attitude of "science," as expressed by practicing scientists as well as philosophers of science, is that science is always unfinished, but there are no limits to what it can discover in the future. The question is whether further progress must lead to either a dualism that defeats physical science, or a complete reductionism that reduces consciousness to an illusion. A third possibility is a development of science that includes and surpasses the present state of science, but which sheds the philosophical assumptions of contemporary materialism.

Koch, for one, offers a proposed direction of science that leaves contemporary materialism behind. He sets out to develop a theory that explains how and why the physical world can generate consciousness. After explaining the concept of "emergence," and asserting that life is an emergent phenomenon of chemistry and physics, he asserts: "Subjectivity is too radically different from anything physical for it to be an emergent phenomenon."[71] The example that he offers to illustrate his point is the experience of a shade of blue, which is radically different from all the electrical activity in the brain of a person who experiences the blue. Although he re-affirms the materialist premise that something such as the perception of a color cannot take place without the activity of the eye's cone photoreceptors, he also acknowledges that the experience cannot be reduced to its physical cause. He takes a giant step, if not a leap, when he states, "I believe that consciousness is a fundamental, an elementary, property of matter."[72] The conventional attitude of most scientists and other modern thinkers is that the elements of the universe are unconscious until evolution accidentally produces an animal with a relatively complex nervous system. [73]

Koch maintains that consciousness is present in all organized pieces of matter. The higher the organization, the greater the consciousness. Consciousness stands as a property of the organization of the elements and cannot be reduced to the elements themselves. According to his thinking, the organized matter need not be organic. Artificial consciousness in complex machines, designed by humans, looms as a distinct possibility.

Along with his late friend and mentor, Francis Crick, Koch attributes his insight to a theory devised by Giulio Tononi called *integrated information*. Tononi's premises are that "Each conscious state is extraordinarily informative, extraordinarily *differentiated* and highly integrated.[74] Consciousness comes with organized chunks of matter. It belongs to the very organization of the system.

Since the word "information" generally means stuff that we know, the deeper scientific and philosophical meaning of the term "information" stands in need of clarification. Koch provides such a clarification beginning with the observation that when we describe every state of consciousness as "informative" we mean that its quality of differentiation makes it absolutely unique so that it can never be repeated. Its uniqueness differentiates it from every other conscious state.

In addition to being differentiated, every conscious state is integrated. We cannot experience components of a state of consciousness apart from the whole. For example, if we are looking at a colorful landscape, we cannot experience it as black and white. While an artist may sketch the landscape using only black pencils, our experience of the sketch would be a different state of consciousness from that of seeing the landscape. If the areas of brain activity, which interact in a state of consciousness, become fragmented, as happens under anesthesia, consciousness fades. Also, if there is little specific information as happens in sleep, consciousness also fades. Consciousness requires a rich supply of differentiated information integrated in a single system. "Any conscious system must be a single integrated entity with a large repertoire of highly integrated states."[75] The implications of integrated information include the affirmation that consciousness constitutes a property of the universe that pervades every integrated system beginning with sub-atomic particles and becoming ever more prevalent in more complex molecules, and more obvious with the evolution of life and higher organisms. Koch connects this conclusion with the ancient belief in pan-psychism, the belief that all matter is to some degree sentient. More specifically, he draws the parallels between integrated information and the belief of the Jesuit paleontologist Teilhard de Chardin (1881—1954), whose law of complexification "...asserts that matter has an inherent compulsion to assemble into ever more complex groupings. And complexity breeds consciousness." [76]

Although Koch affirms that consciousness constitutes a property of the universe that is distinct from matter and that cannot be reduced to matter or an emergent property of matter, he does not deviate from his reductionist stand that consciousness cannot exist without matter. As he sums it up: "But without some carrier, *some mechanism,* integrated information can't exist. Put succinctly: no matter, never mind."

Nevertheless, he affirms a Socratic-like scientific humility reminiscent of William James who said, "Our science is a drop, our ignorance the sea." In Koch's words, "Our knowledge is but a fire lighting up the vast darkness around us, flickering in the wind. So let us be open to alternative, rational explanations in the quest for the sources of consciousness." [77]

Koch's research and his interpretation seem to be more compatible with a teleological than a mechanistic view of the universe. Rather than consciousness being an accidental and insignificant by-product of matter, matter seems to be moving purposively toward the development of consciousness. Although Koch rejects the notion of a soul that can subsist without the brain and also rejects the religious notion of God, he affirms a trust, some might call it a faith, that the universe is not meaningless. Part of this attitude is a faith in science, specifically that it is poised to solve the mind-body problem. But he rejects the temptation to think of science as the final and absolute form of knowledge. "I do not know what will come afterward, if there is an afterward in the usual sense of the word, but whatever it is, I know in my bones that everything is for the best."[78] "I do believe that some deep and elemental organizing principle created the universe and set it in motion for a purpose that I cannot comprehend." [79] If his hunch is right on the last two statements, then consciousness, not human consciousness, but consciousness, has a priority over matter. Not everything is lost with the inevitable disintegration of the physical universe and there is a pathway for dealing with the problem of the good.

As stated at the beginning of this chapter, consciousness while the most universal and familiar of topics, eludes attempts to provide analytical understanding. Yet, consciousness stands out as the most essential condition for anything that we might call good. Materialism reduces consciousness and therefore all good, to an accidental product of blind, indifferent, unconsciousness physical events. But my thesis affirms the reasonableness of holding that consciousness precedes the evolution of the human brain, which becomes a channel of consciousness. If this view, as opposed to the materialist view is correct, then goodness is real and the meaning of our life consists of promoting that which is good aesthetically and ethically. In the following chapters I will strive to show what the priority of consciousness has to do with Biblical religion, how it can also provide meaning for those without religion, and how it enhances our understanding of environmental ethics, economic, and social ethics.

Chapter 5:
Evolution of the Religious Traditions

We have so far reflected on whether consciousness is a rare product of an otherwise unconscious process of physical and biological evolution or whether consciousness is a real power that propels and guides the whole process. The previous chapters described these polar opposites as the materialist and the teleological views. We could simplistically assert that the conflict comes down to atheism versus religion. But the range and depth of possible interpretations is more complex by far. Those who ponder the deeper meaning of reality can move away from the stark materialism of writers like Dennett and Dawkins and still see the whole structure and practice of religion as false and illusory. Those who go deeper may accept the notion of purpose in the process of the evolving universe but still be secularists and even atheists in that they see the notion and name of God as false and misleading. For example, Christof Koch, whose writing I drew from in Chapter Four, sums up his position as a "romantic reductionist" saying: "I do believe that some deep and elemental organizing principle created the universe and set it in motion for a purpose that I cannot comprehend."[80] Koch had rejected traditional religion and affirmed the principle of reductionism, and yet, the above quote affirms a teleological principle.

The Discontinuity between Modern Spirituality and Religion

An often heard phrase states "I am spiritual but not religious." The metaphysical notion of a purpose in the universe can be compatible with science, but does it have any connection with traditional religion? The belief in an anthropomorphic God who cares about and enters human history seems to be an outdated and outlandish superstition compared to the sober reflection of contemporary scientists musing on a possible meaning to the universe. As early as the seventeenth century, regarding the ultimate meaning of the universe, a chasm opened between traditional views on the one hand and rational views on the other. For example, in 1786 future American President, John Adams, who had learned of William Herschel's discovery of the planet Uranus, and the forty-foot long telescope with which he peered into deep space, visited Herschel at his observatory in England. Adams pondered the newly discovered vastness of the universe, the relative insignificance of the earth, and the probability of countless inhabited worlds. He drew the conclusion that the notion of "The Great Principle" becoming human, dwelling on earth, being spat upon and crucified, is absurd, and so Calvinism or any orthodox form of Christianity is a blasphemy that we should get rid of.[81]

In the context of the gap between the religious world-view before the Enlightenment and the science of the last three hundred years, can traditional religion have any standing in the twenty-first century? I will make the case that it can, based on the premise that we human beings are evolving physically, chemically, and biologically toward greater consciousness. As we do so, our understanding of the highest consciousness also evolves, and we can discern a continuity between earlier and later stages. To state this approach in popular theological terms, we gradually come to understand God as revealed over time. As we move toward higher stages of religious awareness, the older and lower stages appear to religious believers as idolatries, and to non-believers as preposterous superstitions.

In tracing the development of religious consciousness, the focus here will be on the Western tradition. While religious consciousness developed independently among people all over the world, and a fruitful encounter among traditions is taking place relatively late in history, this chapter will concentrate on the development that took place, and is still taking place in the Biblical and philosophical traditions of the West.

The Case for Continuity between Religion and Modernity

This section makes the case for a continuity between traditional religion and modern thought by showing an evolution that moves continually, although not smoothly, from the earliest expressions of religion to the theological, ethical, and scientific thinking of our own time. This continuity includes an intimate connection between a world-forming consciousness and the notions and experiences that human beings have with such a consciousness. At first sight the anthropomorphic notions of the Creator, and the religions that have developed around these notions, seem to be so far removed from any feasible scientific explanations as to be useless. In fact, they may be worse than useless in that they stand in the way of rational understanding. But the status of traditional theistic religion deserves and requires a further look, beginning at the beginning. Those of us who have been educated with an acceptance of physical and biological evolution should at least be open to the possibility of spiritual evolution.

Our remote ancestors faced mysterious phenomena that far surpassed their understanding and ability to control. These phenomena included things that are no longer mysteries to us such as the sun moving across the sky, the change of seasons, lightning and thunder, and natural disasters. As consciousness developed, our forbearers projected consciousness on things that we look on as inanimate such as the sun, a holy mountain, or the unseen source of thunder and other phenomena. People faced these seemingly higher realties with a sense of what Rudolph Otto, in his classical work *The Idea of the Holy,* called *Mysterium tremendum and fascionsum.*[82] The mystery appeared to them as overwhelming and at the same time fascinating. They were not yet ready to think philosophically about whatever is the highest power in the universe, but it struck them as extremely powerful and also as fundamentally good. Therefore, they approached and avoided it with a combination of fear and reverence.

In trying to understand the notion of God that has come down to us through the Judeo-Christian tradition, we have to look at the development among the Greeks and the Hebrews. In Western culture, both the popular and the theological notions of God descended primarily from these two sources. A scanning of the development of consciousness in each of these traditions will show the continuity between the early notion of the power behind the universe and an understanding of a divine being that can serve as a live option for scientifically educated people today.

The Greek Tradition

In the Greek tradition, Homer depicts gods and goddesses who were supremely powerful and beautiful and who controlled events on earth from weather conditions to the outcome of battles. These deities were clearly the projection of what humans aspired to or at least wished to be. Most especially, they were immortal. The notion of the gods and goddesses reveals that human consciousness had developed to where people were aware of the tragedy of their mortality, their imperfections, and what they would be if they were not so limited. Significantly, the gods and goddesses did not exhibit a superior morality, and for humans, morality consisted primarily of keeping the deities happy.

The philosopher Xenophanes (570–478 BCE) exhibited a breakthrough in the development of consciousness when he was appalled by the depictions of sleazy morality among the deities and in their treatment of mortals. First, this criticism shows a moral awareness that is not dictated by mythology. Secondly, it shows belief in a non-material consciousness. The gods and goddesses were made after our own image and likeness. Not only were they made to look human, but each ethnic group depicted the deities as looking like those who made the images. Xenophanes argued that God has no body nor is He multiplied according to the multiplication of nations. Aristotle writes of Xenophanes: "with his eye on the whole heaven he says that the one is god."[83]

In *The Republic*, Plato described "The Good" as the source of all good and beautiful forms, which in turn were the source of good and beautiful images in the physical world. The Good is not only above material things; the good is "beyond being." Plato's view represents the complete inverse of any materialism. In the Platonic understanding, the non-physical and invisible reality serves as the source and model for physical reality, which is being called out of chaos into cosmos. In the dialogue *Timaeus,* the title character explaining the reason for creation states:

> God desired that all things should be good and nothing bad, so far as this was attainable. Wherefore also finding the whole visible sphere not at rest, but moving in an irregular and disorderly fashion, out of disorder he brought order, considering that this was in every way better than the other. Now the deeds of the best could never be or have been other than the fairest, and the creator, reflecting on the things which are by nature visible, found that no unintelligent creature taken as a whole could ever be fairer than the intelligent taken as a whole and again that the intelligent could not be present in anything which was devoid of soul.[84]

Timaeus makes it clear that his story should not be taken as an exact account of how the world was created, but only as a probability, which is the most a mortal could hope to achieve. Plato's view of creation, as expressed in *Timaeus*, while not exactly the same as that of a Christian theologian, has much in common with it. Further, Plato's view would fit compatibly with a contemporary religious view of evolution, bringing order out of chaos and seeing intelligence as an essential component of order. The materialist of course sees the ideas of Plato as an illusory invention rather than a discovery of reality.

Aristotle understood God as being above and beyond the natural world, hence the term "metaphysical." For Aristotle, thinking is the highest form of being. Therefore, he describes God, who is pure, fully actualized being, as pure thought thinking of itself.[85] We, as rational animals, are born with the potential to develop the power of rational thought.[86] In his *Nicomachean Ethics,* Aristotle set out to define the highest good for human beings and the means to attain it. At the beginning of the *Ethics* he stipulated that the good is that at which all things aim. Some things are good because they are a means to a higher good; but the greatest good is that which is sought for its own sake. The good of any being consists in achieving its specific *telos*—fulfillment, and since humans are rational animals, our *telos* consists in fulfilling our potential of rationality. In Book X of *Nicomachaen Ethics*, Aristotle recaps the meaning of the best way of life. In Book I, he had identified the good as happiness, defined generally as living well and doing well. Some identify happiness with pleasure, others with honor. But Aristotle contends that the highest happiness consists of contemplation.[87] To the extent that we actualize our potential for thinking and living rationally, we become friends of God; and acquire a virtue that survives the death of our bodily nature.[88] Leaping ahead to the Christian Middle Ages, St. Thomas Aquinas absorbed much of the Aristotelian philosophy and integrated it with Christianity. His synthesis remains a strong force in Catholic thought up to the present.

The Hebrew Scriptures

But while Christian philosophy derived from Aristotle, Christian religion descends from the Hebrew tradition in which God is active and caring in human history, unlike the aloof god of Aristotle. The Hebrew God was revealed to Moses as a mighty warrior-liberator who would force the Egyptians to free the Israelites. But Moses did not understand God as merely a more powerful warrior god among many. God, as revealed to Moses could not be depicted in an image nor could he be invoked by calling his name. In Moses' understanding and teaching, God made a covenant with his people that begins with their liberation from Egypt and the entry into the Promised Land. The duty of the people included exclusive worship of God, who transcended images and names, as well as observance of the required acts of justice to one and other. Setbacks, both before and after their entry in what became their land, were seen as the result of failing to live up to the covenant.

If the evolution of religion, specifically biblical religion, can be seen as the evolution of the human awareness of a transcendent consciousness, the leading edge of this awareness can be found in the person of each of the prophets. In one of the crucial breakthroughs in the history of religion, the prophet Amos upended the notion that we can live a good life simply by placating God with ritual and sacrifice. Amos railed against evil immoral acts and attributed the suffering of the people to God's punishment. But the reform that Amos demanded did not involve pleasing God with rituals. Rather it meant justice toward the poor. Amos, voicing what he believed God said through him, warned:

I hate, I despise your feasts
And I take no delight in your solemn assemblies
Even though you offer me your burnt offerings and cereal offerings,

I will not accept them....
But let justice roll down like water
And righteousness like and ever flowing stream.
Hear this you who trample on the needy

And bring the poor of the land to an end. [89]

American philosopher Josiah Royce (1855 - 1916) summed up the breakthrough of Amos in the context of mediating ideas, which bring together apparently incompatible thought processes. In a previous paragraph, Royce had illustrated the mediating idea of Malthus on the thought of Charles Darwin. Arguing that the same creative process that works in science also works in religion, he showed how Amos reconciled the self-righteousness of religious leaders with the grim reality of the neglected poor. As Royce states it: "Amos introduced into the controversies of his time the still tragic, but inspiring and mediating, idea of the God who, as he declared, delights not in sacrifices but in righteousness. And by this one stroke of religious genius the prophet directed the religious growth of the centuries that were to follow."[90]

So the insight of Amos does not constitute merely another idea in a pantheon of religious ideas. Rather his insight shows real progress. The idea of the need to take care of the poor as central to religion runs through the history of Judaism and Christianity. The tendency to return to a smug selfish attitude remains, but the arrow of religious history shows a constant attempt to overcome greed and selfishness in favor of justice and charity.

The prophetic vision of Amos was carried forward by the prophet Isaiah. As Daniel Berrigan quotes the prophet speaking in the voice of God:

Of what import, what value
These sacrifices of yours,

Innumerable––useless, repugnant!
Turn, turn, turn!
Seek justice,
Succor the oppressed,
Cherish the defenseless![91]

Berrigan observes that the religious sense itself is declared perverted. When religious sense moves forward, the old religiosity, which had been understood as prescribed by God Himself, becomes an obstacle to true worship. This state of affairs can lead to despair. But Berrigan shows the hopeful meaning of this sea change in religious consciousness;

> But just as despair is the ignoble stock-in-trade of the world's systems, hope is the noble stock-in-trade of the prophet. For "my people" some breakthrough, a personal and social change of heart is possible, the prophet is compelled to state this possibility and also to show a path.[92]

Worshiping the supreme reality no longer means placating an angry, jealous, and vengeful despot. Rather it means caring for all human beings in whom consciousness is embodied. To the best of my knowledge, the biblical tradition did not extend compassion to non-human animals as did some forms of Buddhism. This extension is only now coming into western religion.

The Christian Scriptures

The Gospels depict the highest consciousness becoming incarnate in an individual who teaches crowds about the Kingdom of God, which in the context of this thesis would mean individual conscious beings sharing to some extent in the universal world-forming consciousness. The incarnate presence of God was not seen in a warrior, king, or emperor, but in Jesus, a person of no political, economic, or even religious significance. He appealed to the lowest rungs of society. The message seems to be that compared to the universal consciousness, whose essential characteristic is love and compassion, power and wealth fall into insignificance. Lust for power, wealth, and pleasure continue to plague society including the Church. The struggle of evolution as described in Chapter Two goes on in every aspect of human history.

The theme of evolutionary integration struggling with the force of disintegration in the development of religion, can best be shown by examining the Fourth Gospel, "The Gospel According to John," and the writings of St. Paul. To clarify the method of my approach, since I am writing a work of philosophy and not theology or Scripture study, my approach does not begin with Scripture as a source from which we can draw conclusions. Rather, I am beginning with the idea stated in Chapter I, that consciousness precedes matter. The explicit point of this Fifth Chapter is to show continuity between traditional religion and an idea that does not depend on Scripture or on any religious authority. That idea, namely, is that consciousness precedes matter, and in the course of evolution, matter is becoming conscious. If my project is successful, those who study consciousness from the point of view of biology, psychology, or neurology, can also look to religion as a source of insight. It would further mean that those who begin from a religious or theological perspective can find another link to the sciences mentioned here.

St. Paul describes the Christian community as one body and he emphasizes that the community persists by love for Christ and a mutual love of the members for each other. Paul was well aware of the dissension that worked against the communal sense and he spent many of his letters instructing the newly converted Christians to avoid such disunity. For Paul, the acceptance of Christ and his community created a "New Man." But the old habits have a way of returning and exerting themselves. In terms of the theme of this work, the expansion of consciousness to a higher level of love and community co-exists with the old tendency toward egoistic narrowness.

In John's Gospel, the force of light, love, and unity struggles with darkness, hate, and division. Given what we know today about the evolution of our species, we can legitimately interpret these themes as a break-through in consciousness. The development of consciousness requires a greater integration of our brain, which is experienced as a growth in light and love.

The first chapter of John announces that "the light shines in the darkness and the darkness does not overcome it." As we become more conscious, the previous states of consciousness, individual and collective, are judged as darkness. As the popular hymn has it, "I once was blind, but now I see." In Chapter 3 of John, Nicodemus comes to Jesus at night—night connoting darkness. Jesus tells him he must be born anew. At this stage of his life, Nicodemus could understand this statement only as the absurd task of returning to his mother's womb to be born again. Jesus teaches him about being born of the Spirit. This rebirth involves a break-through in consciousness that ordinary consciousness cannot comprehend. Jesus further explains that light has come into the world, but people loved darkness rather than light because their deeds were evil.

Recognition of the light would expose the evil of their deeds. By the time of the New Testament, the consciousness of the human species had developed far beyond anything else on earth. But there was, and is, the tension between the integrating power of consciousness and the disintegrating force of a bodily based individualism.[93] People act out of greed, pride, anger, and hatred in ways that thwart the unifying power of the spirit of consciousness. This idea runs throughout the Gospel, but culminates in the prayer that Jesus offers in Chapter 17:21 "That they all may be one even as thou Father art in me and I in thee, that they all may be one in us." The ultimate goal of the Gospel is the same as and an expression of what I am arguing is the goal of evolution, namely the overcoming of chaos and division and the creation of harmonious integration.

The history of Christianity shows a constant need for reform. The fact that those who consider themselves to be Christians cannot seem to get it right can lead to the conclusion that the enterprise is essentially futile. Maybe those who cling to the notion of a true Christian community should recognize the futility and try something else. In fact, many people in our time have done just that. They turn to secularism, Eastern religion, or spirituality without religion. Those options or a myriad of others might work—work in the sense of providing meaning to life. But the perpetual need for reform does not necessarily mean that the Christian promise is futile.

The awareness of the need for reform indicates a judgment that there can be something better than the status-quo. We sense the need to reform our religion, or any other human institution, when we sense that the reality falls short of what the institution professes to be or what it can potentially be. We cannot think of a need to reform without a vision of the good.

The pull of integrating and dis-integrating forces that run through evolutionary creation exert themselves in the church as elsewhere. The integrating force is the spirit drawing individuals into a community of love. But members easily slip into idolatries of power, wealth, and ethnic exclusiveness. These anti-communal forces then lead to religious wars, persecution, and oppression. The next chapter will deal with how these opposing forces of integration and disintegration play out in the history of the Christian Church.

Chapter 6:
Spirituality and the Church

In previous chapters I have argued for the feasibility of believing that consciousness precedes matter and directs its evolution. In the evolutionary process, matter itself becomes more and more conscious. This development consists of a process of composition in which the infinitely divided elements are becoming integrated. The process takes place in the formation of elements, molecules, stars, and planets. On earth, and probably a multitude of other planets, the process culminates in living organisms, consciousness, and intelligence. In Chapter Five, this process was applied to human religious consciousness. At every step we find the opposition of integration toward greater being and disintegration, which is the tendency to fall back into nothingness. Chapter Six will consider the historical Christian church as a microcosm of the evolutionary struggle.

Evolutionary Struggle in the Church

While the goal of Christianity entails creating the Universal Beloved Community, for two thousand years Christians have frequently fought among themselves or with outsiders. If the premise of this book is correct, the Church, like all human institutions, stands between two opposing forces. These forces consist of the creative action to produce universal harmony, and the contrary tendency to slip back into the all-in-division of nothingness. The first aspect stands out more explicitly in the Church than in any other institution. The Church claims to be the Body of Christ, and therefore the social embodiment of Universal Consciousness. In Christian terminology the highest consciousness is called God, and Christ is called the "Word of God" incarnate. On the other hand, the human individuals who constitute the Church, whether they be hierarchs, clergy, or lay people, weigh themselves down with the disintegrating forces that plague all the human race.

The history of the Church shows a perpetual need for reform. The need stems from the human tendency to slip into forms of idolatry. The idols include power, personal accumulation of wealth, and ethnic exclusiveness. Each of these expresses what I have referred to as forms of disintegration.

In the secular world, a person may legitimately acquire and even accumulate wealth if the purpose is to promote the common good. The wealthy philanthropist can achieve results that the poor philanthropist cannot. Even aside from philanthropy, a wealthy capitalist can promote the prosperity of many through products, jobs, and tax revenue. But those who seek wealth for themselves, regardless of the effect that their action has on others, leave behind dislocations such as lost jobs, environmental deterioration, and an imbalanced use of resources.

So with church officials, wealth can be, and usually is, used for religious, educational, or charitable purposes. But when Church officials slip into the idolatry of wealth and accumulate money for themselves, or to live in a grand style, they present themselves on the wrong side of the evolutionary struggle. Their actions destroy rather than enhance the community. If the persons in power, such as bishops, make power itself their object of worship, and make obedience to themselves the ultimate virtue, they are also destructive of authentic community. Most destructive of all might be the tendency to use religion as a cover to exclude those who are not members of their own community such as people of different religions, ideologies, or sexual orientations.

If the whole evolutionary creative process is to craft a universal community out of an infinitely divided reality, then the duty of religion is to show the way, mainly by example. When religion itself becomes the source of divisiveness, then it has distorted its purpose and become an evil factor.

Creating the Universal Community

Philosopher Josiah Royce saw the credibility of Christianity to lie beyond the historical and accidental features that it acquired during two thousand years. He maintained that if the Church could speak she would say "Create me." He means that the Church exists as an ideal, but an ideal that remains largely unrealized. In describing the origins of the church, he argues that although Christians believe in the words of "The Founder," Jesus, the beliefs and theology of Christianity stem from the *interpretation* of the words and deeds of The Founder, interpretations made by the early Christian community.

The most essential belief is that the community, The Body of Christ, subsists as a reality that transcends the collection of the individuals who compose the community. Further, the individuals find their salvation only in their membership in the community. Royce holds that the experiential discovery of the early Christians constitutes a universal human need. The need is for individuals to realize that their lives are meaningless as long as they remain separated, and that they find their meaning and salvation, only in community. The communities themselves, however, might be separated from each other leading to strife and disintegration. Therefore, the ultimate goal of individuals as well as their communities consists in moving toward a universal community.

Some readers of Royce have been repulsed by the idea of universal community thinking it means universal conformism, or worse, totalitarian authoritarianism. Although these evils have a long and prominent history, and spawned major moral plagues in the twentieth century, they do not constitute what Royce means by a universal community. Rather than conformity in the sense of sameness, the community requires and fosters individual uniqueness. An analogy can help. If bricks are stacked in a pile, each one is essentially like the others. But when builders organize the bricks into an architectural work of beauty, each brick takes on an absolutely unique role, similar to others, but not the same. So in our communities, each of us has a set of relations and a role to play that is unique to each individual. Others may replace us in performing tasks, but they will not duplicate the place that we have in relation to others.

In an authentic community as opposed to a mere collective, each individual enjoys a supreme value precisely as a member of the community. A tyrant, who imposes a total control, ignores the uniqueness and freedom of the individual, and thereby cripples or kills the development of community. This holds true whether the tyranny be in government, religion, business, education, or any other field of human activity.

The Perennial Need for Reform

In every stage of history, people need societal institutions such as church and state to embody and enable human activity and development. But the problem with human consciousness shows up precisely in the fact that it *develops*. Institutions tend to change much more slowly than human consciousness, and those with positions of power in the institutions resist changes that challenge the knowledge and skills that officials spent a life-time learning. Institutions provide stability, which constitutes a human need, but human consciousness continues to evolve. When consciousness becomes incompatible with the dominant institutions, reform or break-up become inevitable. The disconnection between personal consciousness and social institutions spawns many great changes including the Protestant Reformation.

At the time of the Reformation, salvation, for many, meant believing the right doctrines, obeying the rules, and observing the rituals. Most conscientious Christians, including John Calvin and Martin Luther, did all of these things and yet felt inadequate and lost.

They believed that much more was required of them, but they could not achieve it on their own. So they came to the conclusion that salvation comes as an undeserved gift from God. The fact that so many people followed them with such passion indicates that they expressed what people were experiencing but, up until then, could not, or would not articulate.

As stated above, the Church is always in need of reform and renewal. The following will not be a history of reform, but rather a selection of examples to show how the tendency to reform moves in the direction of developing a universal community. The following overview of reform looks at three Catholic reformers, Benedict, Francis of Assisi, and Ignatius of Loyola. This will be followed by a consideration of the Enlightenment, which reformed Christendom by moving away from Christianity. The chapter will close with an assessment of the state of the Christian church within the culture of the twenty-first century.

At the time of St. Benedict (480 - 543), there were many forms of monasticism whose leading characteristic was the attempt to follow a Christian life-style by withdrawing from the prevailing culture of a dying Roman empire. Benedict established a rule that would enable monks to avoid the kind of extremes that withdrawal from the world could spawn, as well as the constant quarreling that dominated much of monastic life.

The motto of the Benedictines was "That in all things God may be glorified" (*Ut in omnibus glorificetur Deus*), and their commitment was to pray and work *(Ora et labora)*. Through their work and example they helped drain the swamps of Europe and promote agriculture. They made Europe a more livable continent and made the faith deeper and more vibrant.

St. Francis would hear the call to reform in the twelfth century. It began for him in an experience of Christ telling him to: "Repair my Church." Francis at first took this literally and began working to repair and clean up church buildings. He would later work to repair the

Church as the community. He did this by imitating the life of Christ as shown in the Gospels and by teaching others to do so. One of the most characteristic features of Christ was poverty. So Francis embraced a life of poverty. Rather than withdrawing from society, he waded into it and taught, by word and example, how people could live as Christians.

St. Francis is known and loved for many things, but perhaps most especially his introduction of the crèche as the symbol of Christ's incarnation. The crèche, which has become a popular part of our contemporary Christmas decorations, depicts Joseph and Mary as a poor couple laying their newborn in a manger in a stable or a cave. The idea of a poor Messiah was not new—it was right out of the Gospels. But it was an idea that Christendom had lost sight of in emphasizing the kingship and divinity of Christ.

St. Ignatius of Loyola came on the scene at a time when the Church was at an especially perilous crossroad. The Protestant Reformation taught that Christians did not need the Catholic Church, and science led many to believe that the human race does not need Christianity in any form. Ignatius developed a company of men who favored both Catholicism and science. St Ignatius and those who followed him, the Jesuits, believed that God can be seen in all of creation. This belief led to an educational system that fostered the study not only of theology and philosophy but also science and humanities. And this belief inspired the Jesuits to travel widely and to appreciate cultures other than their own.

The reforming movements of Luther and Calvin were mentioned above. The Reformation, at first, led to a constant state of war between Catholics and Protestants. Reform does not come easily. But in the twenty-first century, Catholics, Lutherans, and Calvinists no longer see each other as enemies. The same can be said of Christians and Jews. These religious groups willingly learn from each other and work together for common values such as social justice. The notion that there should be only one faith and that all others are wrong, has given way to the idea that a diversity of traditions can nourish the ongoing work of God's creation.

Religion and the Enlightenment

In addition to the Protestant Reformation that moved some Christians away from the Catholic Church, and the reformation within the Catholic Church, western civilization witnessed the Enlightenment, a movement which to a great extent, moved away from traditional religion. Many of those who studied philosophy and the new empirical approach to science, learned that they could discover truths apart from the authority of church officials. My purpose here is not to present a brief history of the rise and development of the Enlightenment, but to call attention to how the Enlightenment exemplifies a move forward in the expansion of consciousness.

The Enlightenment emphasized reason, and the defining characteristic of reason is universality. According their own principles, philosophers cannot expect anyone to accept their ideas based on the authority of the philosopher. Rather, philosophers must present arguments that appeal to the reasoning ability of their audience. In the same manner, scientists must publish the results of their experimental or theoretical findings in ways that can be repeated and understood by other scientists.

Does the emphasis on universality show that science and reason have replaced religion? While there are many who think it does, my contention is that modern thinking does not necessarily replace religion, but enables religion to reform and expand.

As recently as two hundred years ago, our ancestors thought the universe was six thousand years old, and consisted of what we now see as a tiny part of one galaxy. This was a very small parcel of time and space compared to what today's astronomers and physicists are probing. While the magnificence of the scientific world-view might meet the needs that religion formerly met, religious believers who are cognizant of science can have a view of creation much richer than was available to their ancestors.

Some religious believers and some scientists might continue to quarrel, while others see science and religion as two separate parallel paths, which neither harm nor help each other. But another, and I think much wiser approach, appreciates science as a way to deeply enrich religious consciousness.

Theologian John Haught uses the term convergence to describe ways that science and faith can be mutually supportive.[94] According to convergence, although science and theology constitute different aspects of reality, theology can develop and grow as it learns more about the natural world from a developing science. Neither faith nor science can provide the content of the other. Further, a religious believer need not be a scientist, and a scientist need not be a religious believer. But a person can be both religious and scientific, and each area can enrich the other. The most recent discoveries of science can help the religious person see creation as a narrative with the best still ahead of us. Religion can give science a justification of the faith that all scientists need, a faith that the universe is ultimately lawful, predictable, and intelligible.

Outcome of this Interpretation

After presenting the Church as a microcosm of the evolutionary struggle, what can we conclude about the role of the Church now and in the future? In a sense, the evolutionary struggle is not just something of value, it is the only thing of value. I have tried to show that consciousness precedes matter and that everything that we call physical reality consists in the process by which consciousness becomes expressed in matter. So the evolutionary struggle consists of the conflict between the movement toward the greatest integrity of elements that would allow the experience and expression of consciousness. The process involves conflict because the parts resist integration and constitute a movement of disintegration. This process plays out in everything from the physical formation of stars and planets, to the evolution of life, to the development of science, to order and justice within nations, to international order and justice. The Church also stands as part of the process. It has a special role because it claims to embody the universal community. But since the Church consists of individual human beings, the tendency to resist unity persists and so there is a constant need for reform. The role of the Church is to keep alive the ideal of the community that all reality strives to become.

Chapter 7:
Spirituality for the Great Un-churched

For many people in the twenty-first century, belief in God is not a live option. Many of the non-believers may be caught up in the search for personal pleasure, wealth, or power; but the same can probably be said of many who profess belief. On the other hand, many non-believers work for the universal community in fields such as science, art, protecting nature, and community development. Josiah Royce describes such people as members of the "invisible church" and sees them as co-workers with authentic Christians in building the Beloved Community. If Royce, and the premise of this work are correct, then these non-believers also find their highest good in the beloved community.

Science as a Higher Purpose

Science can be a path to membership in the universal community, even for atheists. In Chapters Five and Six, I tried to show a continuity between historical religion and a science-informed understanding of the principles of the universe. But here I will try to show how a person can come to spiritual maturity through universal principles even though traditional religion may not be a live option.

While I maintain that belief in a purposeful Creator serves as the most rational foundation for a scientific understanding of the universe—such was Albert Einstein's belief—I know that many scientists can dispense with the metaphysical underpinning, and make scientific knowledge itself the foundation of a meaningful life. Examples abound such as Sean Carroll with his "Poetic Naturalism," and Kristof Koch with his "Romantic Reductionism." This group also includes many of the most famous scientists of our time, such as Stephen Hawking and Francis Crick.

Several reasons can help explain why many scientists eschew religion and metaphysics. First, science, especially physics, has replaced both religion and philosophy as the road to understanding reality. Second, the mind of a scientist tends to reject that which is not amenable to scientific verification or falsification. Third, science meets the deepest need for meaning, and for those who find such meaning, philosophy or religion can only get in the way.

The first of the reasons stated above, that physics better answers the questions that earlier generations expected of religion and philosophy, is true. When Napoleon asked Pierre Simon Laplace (1749 -1827) why he didn't mention God in his work on celestial mechanics, Laplace answered, "I had no need of that hypothesis."[95] Questions about the origin, development, and composition of the natural world are best left to science. Religious believers who attempt to use religious sources such as Scripture to answer these questions make a huge mistake that harms both science and religion. Those who would use the Bible to explain the origin of life, for example, miss out on what they might learn from evolution as well as the real spiritual meaning of the biblical passages. Scientists who think that the Bible is an unscientific alternative to these questions also miss out on the meaning of the biblical passages, but at least they have their science.

A further reason that many scientists reject or ignore religion is that their training and practice leads them to disdain questions that cannot be answered by possible empirical verification or falsification.[96] William James, a seminal thinker in science and religion, observed in 1906 that scientists often close themselves off to any possible awareness of the transcendent, not because their scientific knowledge gives them a clearer understanding of reality, but because their critical attitude prevents them from ever accessing any aspect of reality that they cannot understand. In James's words:

> Relatively few medical men and scientific men, I fancy, can pray. Few can carry on any living commerce with "God." Yet many of us are aware of how much freer and abler our lives would be, were such important sources of energy not sealed up by the critical atmosphere in which we have been reared... One part of our mind dams up––even *damns* up––the other parts. [97]

Scientists and other critical thinkers who reject any idea that is not an object, or at least a potential object, of empirical investigation, often see this rejection as a strength. They find meaning in their courageous adherence to their strict rules of evidence. Such commitment, along with the fascinating study of science and other fields of learning may satisfy all of their spiritual needs.

For many of the skeptics mentioned in the previous paragraph, thinking about things for which there is no scientific evidence is, at best, a waste of time. At worst it is an apostasy to the belief that science, as it exists today, is the only path to understanding reality. Although there still may be countless unanswered questions, these skeptics see no need for any way of asking these questions other than that of science.

A relevant article by Peter Atkins, which appeared on-line in *Aeon*, 8 -21-2018, argues that since science has proved itself reliable in answering all kinds of questions about the physical world, perhaps its ability to understand reality is unlimited. He points out that science is driven by a kind of optimism in its method for providing answers to the biggest questions that can potentially be clarified by evidence. He rejects the intellectual legitimacy of questions that are not potentially answered by scientific evidence. In dismissing those "invented questions" that are based on unwarranted extrapolations from human experience he says:

They typically include questions of purpose and worries about the annihilation of the self, such as *Why are we here?* and, *What are the attributes of the soul?* They are not real questions, because they are not based on evidence. Thus, as there is no evidence for the Universe having a purpose, there is no point in trying to establish its purpose or to explore the consequences of that purported purpose.

He concludes that questions of this nature as well as any questions about a "soul" are meaningless and have no answer. [98]

In this chapter, I am not presenting counter-views to materialism; I have tried to do that in other chapters. Here I am trying to show that membership in the great community need not be closed to those whose beliefs do not go beyond materialism. Scientific materialists can discover a community of truth-seekers with their fellow scientists and a sense of cosmic community as they discover or learn about the ways in which the human mind can comprehend the working of the universe. A well-articulated proposal for science as the source for human meaning comes from theoretical physicist, Sean Carroll, in his 2016 book, *The Big Picture.* Carroll proposes what he calls "poetic naturalism" as a way for scientists and scientifically informed people to find meaning in an otherwise meaningless universe.

Carroll defies "naturalism" as the belief that there is only one world, the natural world. The poetic part of the idea refers to our way of talking about the everyday world.[99] Although there are "no reasons why" in the deep workings of nature itself, we may speak meaningfully of reasons as if they were real. We need to reflect on the best way of living without any help from outside of our understanding of nature. Since we live with other people, we have to work together to find the best way for all of us to live together. Carroll emphasizes freedom and responsibility. A person can reasonably agree with Carroll that in reality, purpose and free will do not exist, but that we can speak and act as if they were real. Or we can disagree with Carroll and hold that there is purpose and free will. We can agree that physical science constitutes the best and most reasonable way of talking about physical reality, but still maintain that it does not exhaust the full potential of human understanding. If matter precedes consciousness, then purpose and free will are illusions. But if consciousness precedes matter, purpose and free will can be real, and so can the content of physical science.

Meaning in Art

In addition to science, materialists can find deep meaning in art. Those who believe in a spiritual reality, the primacy of consciousness, can see art as a connection and tapping into a transcendent beauty. But the materialists, who maintain that the world, as understood by physics, constitutes the whole of reality, can also find meaning in art. They see the artist as creating a beauty that otherwise does not exist. They find even greater meaning if they themselves are able to create. I'm using the term art here in its broadest sense to include not only visual art but also music, poetry, literature, drama, landscaping, dance, cooking, and anything else that provides meaning to human beings.

What the materialists and the teleologists have in common is the conviction that art lifts our experience not only above the chaotic strife of the everyday struggle for existence, but also above the mundane world that usually passes for reality. In this section, I am not offering a theory of the meaning of art—it has several meanings––but I will try to show how those who hold to a materialistic view of reality can find an experience of the good by means of art.

To clarify my thoughts on what art might mean for a materialist, I will compare it to what art means to some of those whom I have been calling teleologists. If consciousness precedes matter, as I have been arguing throughout this work, the creation of the universe consists of bringing matter out of nothingness, through chaos, and into order. For us human beings, whose lives express much chaos, there looms a vague awareness of and yearning for order. The characteristics of order include harmony, balance, and wholeness. When these qualities show up in visible matter, we experience them as beauty. Of course, natural as well as artistic beauty exceeds the three qualities mentioned above, and may evoke emotions such as compassion, reverence, and love, including erotic love.

As we evolve, both as a species and as individuals, we become more conscious and, therefore, more aware of and more appreciative of the good and its manifestation in the form of beauty. For the teleologists, the experience of beauty is a hint of what lies ahead for us and what attracts us and urges us forward. The materialists may experience the same beauty, but see it as something that comes from human consciousness and that will perish along with human consciousness, but makes the process more enjoyable and bearable.

Teleologists and materialists differ in their understanding of where the beauty of art comes from. Here I will remind the reader that I am using the term teleologists to refer to anyone who believes that the universe has purpose. Although it includes most religious believers, it is not limited to those who believe in or practice organized religion. But the teleologist believes that the human creator of beauty taps into a higher reality and embodies it in images, buildings, music, or words. To cite one example, the twentieth century Cistercian monk and spiritual writer Thomas Merton describes the architecture of the early Cistercians:

> The reason Cistercian architecture was what it was, was not that the Cistercians tried to start a new technique, but our Order was built and grew up as an organic whole, out of the basic and all-consuming desire for a perfectly pure love of Him.[100]

According to Merton, the architecture was a physical and visible expression of the spiritual love of the monks for God. The style cannot be reproduced by those who do not experience the same spiritual reality. A materialist, by contrast, would see artistic beauty as a new but temporal expression of the artist. From this point of view, there is no eternal or spiritual reality.

The fact that experience of beauty dissolves so easily and we humans sink back into chaos in our actions as well as the way we treat our surroundings seems to favor the materialist viewpoint. Compassion gives way to strife, reverence to arrogance, and erotic love to sexual excess. The problem of evil, dealt with in Chapters Two and Three, returns. I will not repeat the defense of the good here, but will simply point out the obvious fact that whether things are becoming better, worse, or the same, art can furnish meaning for many people, including materialists.

Meaning in Human Relationships

In addition to science and art, personal relations constitute another non-religious way in which we can make life meaningful. Examples of such relationships range from one-on-one encounters to communities, nations, the whole human race, and the whole biosphere.

A good example of finding meaning through a one-on-one relationship can be seen in Matthew Arnold's "Dover Beach." Arnold was not a materialist, but he understood the worldview of those who no longer could hold to any faith and had not found anything to replace it. The poet describes love as the one flicker of hope in a sea of despair:

Ah, love, let us be true
To one another! For the world, which seems
To lie before us as a land of dreams.
So various, so beautiful, so new,
Hath really neither joy, nor love, nor light

Nor certitude, nor peace, nor help for pain.

The narrator hears only the "note of eternal sadness" and the "long withdrawing roar" of the Sea of Faith. Surely most teleologists hear the same note of eternal sadness and feel the despair. But they can see the fidelity of the lovers as a glimpse of an infinitely larger reality. However, like all good things in life, love and friendship struggle with the tendency of all finite things to disintegrate, while at the same time they serve as beacons showing the way, and as lived examples of the teleological harmony that constitutes the ultimate good. The love itself becomes the cause to which both lovers are loyal and are able to be true to one another.

What Secularists Have to Say

Science, art, and personal relationships, among other things, can serve to provide meaning for secularists. In this section I will cite a prominent philosopher who rejects the notion of a cosmic purpose but who offers a meaningful approach to life. If he is successful, and if my attempt to interpret him is successful, the possibility that a person can live a meaning-filled life even in the absence of cosmic purpose could lead to several different conclusions, of which I will cite two opposing views.

The materialists can argue that since human life can be meaningful even while holding to the primacy of matter, then the notion that consciousness has priority is illusory and superfluous. The teleologists can counter that the materialists are able to benefit from their relation to a transcendent consciousness, even though their metaphysics cannot account for it. I will not even try to adjudicate this issue, but instead will cite the thoughts of a meaningful materialist.

One philosopher who makes a good case for meaning without any spiritual reality is Michael Ruse. In his book, *On Purpose,*[101] Ruse argues that a non-religious person can live a purposeful life. His position presents several problems for my thesis. I was presenting a contrast between a materialist and a teleological view of things, and arguing that purpose implies the priority of consciousness over matter. Ruse rejects the notion of a universal purpose, but holds that living things do in fact have values and therefore purpose. He cites Darwinism as his guiding principle and also suggests that a primitive consciousness might inhere in all of matter. If this last hypothesis is true, then there is no ontological break between matter and mind.

Ruse expresses his opinions with a caution against taking positions that run ahead of science. He readily admits what he does not know, but affirms views that at least coincide with established science. The outcome of his thinking, as of the time he wrote *On Purpose,* consists of an affirmation of what he calls "modified panpsychism." He rejects as "looniness" the notion that plants, much less, molecules, can think. But he assents to the view that "there is something about molecules that gives rise to thinking."[102] In his view the difference between a molecule and a thinking organism is one of increment rather than innovation. His position differs from both sides of the dichotomy of consciousness and matter that make up the theme of this work. He would, in practical terms, come closer to the materialist side, holding that the molecules that give rise to consciousness precede full-blown consciousness. He affirms that the next couple of centuries might reveal things to our descendants that would surprise all of us.

Ruse spends a chapter presenting a polemic against religion, but begins his final chapter dealing with the possibility of purpose without God. According to Ruse, Christianity and religion generally find meaning primarily, if not only, in the afterlife. Because Ruse rejects the idea of an afterlife, he concludes that if meaning is to be found at all, it must be found here and now. Further, in rejecting the idea of God, Ruse not only rejects the biblical idea, but the reality of universal consciousness or anything that might be called "spiritual." He argues against the notion that there is purpose in evolution or in human history. The heart of his thesis comes in his discussion of individual purpose.

In presenting his own life as an example of how we can find values without any foundation other than Darwinism, Ruse cites three area in which he has found meaning value and purpose. The first of these is family and friends. He presents a vivid description of his own marriage and parenthood as a happy time, and emphasizes the importance of a sense of humor to deal with the imperfections. In addition to family, he refers to friends and alludes to Aristotle, who considered friendship to be an essential component of any happy life.

The second area in which Ruse finds value is in service. He cites his Quaker background for the original motivation, but his own service was mainly in his career: teaching, mentoring, writing, and editing. I don't know any of his students, but anyone who reads his books can appreciate his contribution.

Finally, like most professors and writers, he considers the life of the mind to be an arena for achieving meaning and purpose. From his earliest childhood, he has been a voracious reader and combines a vast understanding of literature to his main interest in philosophy, biology, and especially Darwinism. Further, he aspired to be not only a knowledgeable spectator, but also a player in the life of the mind. To this end he describes how, whenever he was bored, say at department meetings, he would tune out and plan a book. This led to a prodigious output of non-fictional authorship.

If my thesis is correct, that consciousness precedes matter, then the meaningful aspects of life that Ruse cites would be a matter of course. We find meaning in family and friends because we share a common consciousness in which each of us expresses a unique part. Service to others follows naturally from recognizing our common source. Such is the meaning of the command to "love your neighbor as yourself." In a real sense, your neighbor is yourself. Ruse acknowledges that he learned the importance of service from his Quaker upbringing. And finally, the life of the mind stands out. If consciousness precedes matter, then our natural imperative is to grow in knowledge and wisdom as well as in love. A mindful religious person, like a mindful secularist, will find these meanings here and now.

Since not everyone can share my idea that consciousness precedes matter, and I am not likely to convince anyone who is dedicated to materialism or any kind of reductionism, it is reassuring to know that those who disagree with me may also find a purposeful life. Most people, hopefully, can find some meaning in family and friends. The idea of service to others stands at least as an option for most. Few people, religious or secular, have a life of the mind to match that of Michael Ruse. But all of us can find meaning in some favored area of reading and learning. Further, we can engage in mindful pursuits such as following a favorite sports team, or pursuing hobbies such as golf, fishing, or woodworking. Although I have argued that my thesis best deals with the "problem of the good," I am glad that those who reject my position can still pursue and enjoy the good.

Chapter 8:
Spirituality, Economics, and Ecology

Economics and the Problem of the Good

What do the preceding chapters have to say about the activity at which most people spend the greatest amount of their time and energy, the activity of providing food, clothing, shelter, and other material goods for themselves and their families? We call the things that we produce and consume "goods." But environmentalists remind us that in the process we also produce bads. The bads include environmental pollution and destruction, depletion of resources, and products that are harmful to people and to the ecological integrity of localities or even to the whole biosphere.

In Chapter One, I offered an idea of the Good that differs from the contemporary materialism, and I have tried to apply this idea to each of the chapters. To repeat the non-materialist key idea: "An alternative vision sees the universe as a process of moving from absolute chaos to a cosmos that expresses order, beauty, harmony, consciousness, freedom, joy, and love." So, applying this idea, first to our economy and then to the larger natural environment, we can begin by considering a world like Thomas Hobbes' "war of each against all,"[103] and discern how we move toward an economic community as described in the previous paragraph.

Evolution, Liberty, and Social Justice

The burden of this chapter consists of showing how the idea of the good as presented in the earlier chapters applies to a morally good economy. We began with the idea that creation consists of reality moving from total chaos of all-in-division, to cosmos, which means all-in-unity. This process can be seen in everything from the formation of molecules through the evolution of species to the development of modern economies.

Applying these ideas to our economy, we can see that through all of prehistory and most of history, the vast majority of people did not make economic decisions. People almost always worked and made a living based on the geographical and societal situation in which they found themselves. Peasants worked land that they did not own, members of fishing and hunting tribes and communities worked as their parents and ancestors did. But more recently, the unprecedented changes in the modern era meant that people were compelled to change both their geographical location and their way of working. For many this meant moving from rural to urban areas and learning to do work other than what their families had previously done. For many, it meant crossing an ocean to a land with a strange language and customs, and to perform work that they had never done before. In the case of Africans, the move was involuntary, forced, and brutal. Today, a lot of people are uprooted and they change locations and types of work several times within one life. This chapter will deal with our contemporary situation, specifically with living and working in the United States.

Thinking about economics and spirituality includes both our attitude toward public policy and our individual choices concerning production and consumption of material goods. Some argue that public policy should involve nothing more than preventing force and fraud and that the free market can take care of how goods are produced and distributed. Others hold that the government should be proactive in establishing and preserving social justice. Of course, there is much disagreement as to what constitutes social justice and what exactly the role of government ought to be.[104]

Before evaluating the various views of freedom and social justice, I will briefly state the relation between biological and social evolution. In biological evolution, molecules, which are a complex arrangement composed of atoms, become integrated into more complex cells, tissues, organs and organisms that work in harmony for the survival of the organisms and their species. Although some interspecies relationships are cooperative, organisms often become hostile to organisms of other species who consist of their predators or their prey. Within a species, organisms may compete with each other for food, territory, or mates. The horrors of natural selection as a mechanism of evolution, which some see as proof of a purposeless universe, are described in Chapter Two.

We can see our economy, initially, as a collection of individuals each looking out for his or her own good. Adam Smith had famously said that we receive our meat, bread, and beer, because the butcher, baker, and brewer are each seeking his own self-interest. This idea inspires libertarians who agree with Ayn Rand that "selfishness is a virtue" and that the unfettered market provides the best arrangement for the production and distribution of economic goods. According to the Libertarians, the role of government should be limited to preventing force and fraud. Ayn Rand called this arrangement "Capitalism—The Unknown Ideal." Capitalism in reality, however, is much more complex than it appears in Ayn Rand's fiction. In the following I will lay out the case for an unfettered capitalism, the case against it, and then see how the conflicting ideals can be reconciled in terms of evolution to a more integrated society.

The Case for Capitalism

Defenders of capitalism cite freedom as one of its main advantages. In addition to being an indispensable condition for human happiness and flourishing, freedom leads to a higher standard of living. The reason is that, in a free economy, anyone who has an idea for a product or service that other people want is free to produce it as long as he or she can do so at a price that people are able and willing to pay. Like Adam Smith's butcher, baker, and brewer, the entrepreneurs may enrich the material lives of those who want and can afford their product. Inventing, producing, pricing, and marketing the product are done out of self-interest, but must adjust to the needs and wants of the potential customers. There is never a guarantee of success, but there is the opportunity to try. The ones who succeed add to the material wealth of their society.

Further, the producers must correctly judge what the consumers want and what they are willing to pay. And they must be alert to changes in the market and be ready to adjust accordingly. Those who judge wrong will lose, others will win. In this way the market imitates biological natural selection. Hence the term "Social Darwinism." The free market capitalists argue that if government tries to intervene in order to mitigate suffering, they would have the same effect as a wrong-minded interfering in biological evolution. If humans killed all the predators out of pity for the prey, the population explosion of herbivores would destroy the environment. Those who defend pure capitalism often reject social justice as an unwarranted and harmful interference in the natural progress of wealth creation.

A further advantage of capitalism beyond the promotion of freedom and entrepreneurship, is that accumulation of capital stands as a necessary condition for the creation of wealth. Economists understand capital as wealth that can be used to create more wealth, for example, factories, equipment, railroads and such. Of course, the state could build and run these things. Some commentators such as the Yugoslav writer, Milovan Djilas, defined the economy of the old Soviet Union not as Socialism, but as "State Capitalism." States can produce large quantities of material things, especially in terms of military equipment, but they lack an effective mechanism for knowing what the population needs and wants.

The ideal of Capitalism conforms to the goal of an integrated society. A market economy requires mutual respect, an absence of violence and fraud, and it requires a rule of law. Therefore, to the extent that people support Capitalism and a market economy, the community described in the previous chapters is supported and enhanced.

The Case against Unbridled Capitalism

While the previous paragraphs laid out the advantages of Capitalism as an ideal, the problems that have been generated by actual historical Capitalism abound. One widespread problem with capitalism occurs when those in charge of corporations put profit-maximization ahead of the long-range purpose of the business. For example, if windfalls from such things as tax-cuts are used to buy the company's own stock, this will enrich those who own the stock, a group that notably includes the executives who are making the decisions. But the common good, as well as the long-term good of the business is better served if the money is used for research and development, as well as wages that will enable the company to recruit and maintain a stable, loyal, and competent work-force.

The problems associated with capitalism become most acute when wealthy individuals or corporations acquire "ownership" of land. The term "ownership" was put in scare quotes because ownership of land is very problematic. The classical definition of private property, as formulated by John Locke, attributes ownership to labor. If anglers, fishing legally, catch some game fish, the fish belong to them by virtue of their labor and skill. But they do not thereby own the lake or stream. The trout fisherman did not create the stream, and neither the deer-hunter nor the logger created the wooded land.

In the time before Locke, all the land, including lakes and forests, belonged to the king. He could determine how much use his subjects could make of these natural resources. In a democratic society, these resources belong to all the people. Our predecessors determined that some land could be managed best by private ownership. So homesteaders were given one hundred sixty acres. But ownership of land does not mean that the owners can do anything they want.

We generally look on private ownership of a home and the lot on which it is situated as a good thing for the owner and the community. A live-in owner is more likely to invest in up-keep such as painting and repairs than is a renter or absentee landlord. Further, homeowners do not worry about someone selling the property and evicting them. But homeowners often must obey restrictions. For example, in most residential communities, homeowners may not choose to raise pigs in their backyard or to rent out their upstairs as a brothel.

The same principle holds for privately owned businesses. A restaurant cannot sell alcohol without a license; a drug store must follow state laws pertaining to the dispensation of habit-forming medications. Although there may be some libertarians who think people should be allowed to do whatever they want, as long as it does not involve force or fraud, the vast majority of citizens, liberal and conservative, believe that some regulation is necessary for the common good.

In most of the developed countries of the world, including the United States, large corporations are privately owned but are subject to regulation. The public sector should not interfere with business except in cases in which the common good, or the basic rights of individuals are concerned. The areas that come under regulation include worker safety, consumer safety, fair treatment of employees, and environmental considerations.

Economic Justice and Integrity

Any person's concept of justice is based on his or her concept of *what a human being is* and why we should be concerned with treating each person justly. We are naturally communal and our capacity for membership in any genuine community rests on the fact that we are rational, free, capable and in need of meaningful work, and needing the opportunity to realize our full physical, intellectual, emotional, and spiritual capacity. Therefore, any structure or practice that inhibits a person from realizing his or her human nature is unjust, and that which promotes it is just. Justice as a moral task can mean doing whatever we can to assure that each person has an opportunity to realize his or her human potential. This entails much more than removal of obstacles, such as discrimination. Real equality of opportunity must include providing the conditions that make realization possible. If a person has the ability and desire to develop productive skills, but lacks the opportunity, does this not constitute an injustice? The role of justice lies in determining what each person has the right to and who has the obligation to provide it.

The theme of this work contends that the good consists of integrity and integration of all the parts. In the case of economic issues, the parts are the individuals and the whole is the economy on which they all depend. The integration in this case can be called social justice and the key to understanding social justice consists in recognizing that we are mutually interdependent. Each of our lives has an impact on countless people of whom we are not aware, and the activities of other people impact each of us. No one in isolation and relying on only his or her own native ability can become an engineer, an accountant, a steamfitter, a golfer, or a musician. All of these things require physical and social structures and involve imitation and intense education, both formal and informal. While those who deny social justice may agree that we have an obligation as individuals to people whom we immediately affect, our universal mutual interdependence requires us to also pay attention to how we collectively impact other people through our political, economic, educational, and civil institutions.

Any society that excludes some part of the population, either by design or by neglect, to that extent suffers a deficiency of justice. Although giving a person a handout, by the state or by private charity, beats letting the person starve or freeze, such largess falls short of justice. The goal of achieving a just society requires that we, individually and collectively, do what we can to assure that each person can take a productive social and economic role. To achieve this level of inclusiveness would be very difficult, if not practically impossible. Nevertheless, it is a standard against which we can measure our level of success and failure at building a just society.

The progress toward good consists of the ever greater harmonious integration of parts. In describing social justice, we are describing the integration of individuals in society. We can rate our society as a just society to the extent that each and every individual has a place in the society that enables them to develop their full human potential. There will probably always be misfits, sociopaths, and criminals. The question of social justice requires that we ask whether we are giving each sufficient opportunity to be productive and prosperous, and how we treat those who reject or neglect the opportunities that are provided. Whether their problem is physical, psychological or moral, they still belong to the human community. We can move to seek ways to incorporate them, although there is no guarantee of success. Or we can reject or neglect them with the self-assurance that their problem is their fault, not ours. As in every aspect of ethics, we can integrate or disintegrate.

Spirituality and Ecology

The discussion in this chapter has so far concerned itself with the process of integrating our own thoughts, our lives, and our relationships in our economic world. The following will develop the theme as it appears in our understanding of the natural world, and most specially, the world of living things.

The very word "ecology" from *oikos*-home and *logos*—reasoning, shows that those who pursue this study recognize the natural world as a home, not a vast meaningless place where species battle for survival, and that there is a basis for rational understanding of our home. In unfolding the relation between human consciousness and matter in the area of ecology, I will start with the relatively late period that we call modernity

At the beginning of the modern era, Rene Descartes (1596 - 1650) distinguished two kinds of substance, which we generally refer to as mind and matter. Although not many philosophers or scientists after him claimed to be his followers, they most often held to the split of mind and matter. The world and all living things including the human body were seen as an object of study for the human mind. The dominant model was the machine, and the human mind applied the laws of mechanics to all physical reality. Descartes' goal of making human intelligence the master and possessor of nature became the guiding principle of the modern age. This relationship was expressed in almost every aspect of our culture but especially in science, technology, and industrialization.

One alternative to the dualism described here, was materialism. According to materialism there is one kind of reality, physical reality, which acts according to the laws of physics and chemistry. Not only the human body, but even what we call mind can be explained by electro-chemical processes in the brain. This was discussed in the opening chapter of this book. But whether the attitude toward the human mind is one of dualism or materialism, the non-human world is seen as an object to be mastered and possessed.

Environmental Ethics

In the second half of the twentieth century a developing environmental ethics served to awaken us to the intrinsic value of the non-human world, to the value of beauty, creation, and enchantment. In trying to reconstruct our ethical attitude, environmental ethics has given us a viewpoint from which we can begin to integrate nature into our ethical world. Of course artists, poets, philosophers, and naturalists had found beauty and spiritual nourishment in nature for some time before the twentieth century. The appreciation of nature can be seen especially in the movement known as Romanticism, which began in the late eighteenth century as a reaction to rationalism of the modern era.[105]

In 1947, Aldo Leopold published *A Sand County Almanac,* in which he set out to develop a "land ethic." He argued that ethics develops over time and always involves the relations of individuals with each other and with their social organizations. The historical development of ethics entails the expansion of areas of conduct governed by a sense of right and wrong. He shows examples of these expansions in the Mosaic Decalogue, the Golden Rule, and the emergence of political democracy.[106] The relation of human individuals to each other and to our organizations became more and more inclusive. But land is considered as mere property and not a part of life governed by ethical considerations.

Leopold believed that the next crucial stage in ethical development entails thinking of land, not as a commodity, but as a community deserving love and respect. Leopold defined the guiding principle of a land ethic. "A thing is right when it tends to preserve the integrity, stability, and beauty of the biotic community. It is wrong when it tends otherwise."

Reverence for our Relations with Non-Human Nature

The consequence of the modern anthropocentric utilitarian view has been a tendency to pinch rather than develop our consciousness. We look at nature acquisitively and ask "What's in it for us?" instead of looking at it contemplatively and asking "What is it?" We might expect traditional religion to be a countervailing force against the lack of reverence for nature. Economist E. F. Schumacher held that economics that acted as if the earth mattered would be a Buddhist economics in traditionally Buddhist countries such as Burma, but a Christian economics in Europe and the United States. But even Christian thought has to a large extent succumbed to the modern reduction of the non-human world, in spite of the Gospel observation that the Creator cares about every sparrow. The progress of consciousness does not constitute a straight line. The exclusive anthropocentrism of the enlightenment contrasts sharply with an earlier natural law theory. St. Thomas Aquinas, for example, stated "God's goodness could not be adequately represented by one creature alone. God produced many and diverse creatures so that what was wanting to one in the manifestation of divine goodness might be supplied by another"[107] By contrast, the contemporary neglect of the intrinsic goodness of the non-human world coincides with a shallow understanding of our own inner world. When the outer world is reduced to an object of quantitative calculation, the human is reduced to a calculator. As E. F. Schumacher observed, all traditional wisdom emphasizes self-knowledge as a condition for knowledge and the love of others:

> The Christian (and other) saints knew themselves so well that they could "see into" other beings. The idea that St Francis could communicate with animals, birds, and even flowers, must of course seem incredible to modern men who have so neglected self-knowledge that they have difficulty communicating even with their wives. [108]

Farmer philosopher, Wendell Berry, in describing what he names "the sin of abstraction" argues that the Devil's work is found not in love of material things but in a love of quantification. A real lover of the material world would not sacrifice the natural environment by making profit maximization the only moral goal; the lover of quantification would.[109] Perhaps we can put a finer edge on Berry's point by saying that the sin is not quantification but reductionism that leaves out everything except quantification. The materialism discussed in the opening chapters of this book naturally leads to quantification. An appreciative knowledge of nature requires that we understand a living relationship between the natural world and ourselves as natural and conscious beings.

Berry, in developing a Christian approach to environmental care, cites the Buddhist notion of right livelihood and contends that Christianity has so far been inadequate in giving us a sense of right livelihood. Sometimes Christian thought has slipped into a dualism that sees the natural world as dead matter. My theme describes the whole evolutionary process as consciousness more and more expressing itself in the natural world. Berry argues that the depreciation of matter stems from the emphasis on other-worldliness. Christianity sees charity as a gift of God, but as Berry points out, we need to learn how to put charity into practice. Speaking from the view point of a farmer he asks; "How can you love your neighbor if you don't know how to build or mend a fence, how to keep your filth out of his water supply, and your poison out of his air?" He gives some suggestions of right livelihood.

> Real charity calls for the study of agriculture, soil husbandry, engineering, architecture, mining, manufacturing, transportation, the making of monuments and pictures, songs and stories. It calls not just for skill but for the study and criticism of skills, because in all of them a choice must be made: they can be used either charitably or uncharitably.[110]

It is clear that the charitable or desirable way to do each of these enhances the good of yourself, your neighbor, and the land on which all of us depend. To know exactly what constitutes the best requires careful study and criticism with an eye to the totality of our good and bad effects, and not just on the one narrow good of profit-making.

This does not mean that we owe all living things the same respect that we should show to humans or even to higher animals. A reasonable criterion for an ascending scale is the quality of consciousness that each organism can experience. We are not acting wantonly when we put our needs above the needs of other animals and plants as in eating food or combating disease. But we must recognize that living things have an intrinsic value that does not depend on whether or not they serve human wants and needs. We cannot live and "do no harm." But we can strive to minimize harm and to live with a sense of reverence and gratitude toward the living things that sustain us.

Our growing consciousness and quest for a universal harmony requires us to support public policy that protects and improves both the land and the people. Since technology moves constantly, the best ideas as to how to protect the land and the people will have changed from the time of this writing to the time that you are reading it. Therefore, it would not be appropriate to speculate on the exact way in which activities such as our use of energy ought to change. Currently it is not clear what will be the best way to power our production of electricity or our transportation, although it seems clear that we will want and need sources of power for both of these activities.

We might cling to the current practice of burning massive amounts of fossil fuel until the system breaks down completely. If the analysis presented in this chapter is correct, then finding and implementing more environmentally friendly production and use of energy ought to be a priority of the government of the United States as well as that of all national governments.

Since war contributes so much to pollution and destructive use of resources, along with the massive destruction of life and the unspeakable grief that it imposes on populations, avoiding and preventing war remains at the top of ethical imperatives. The technology for achieving a significant reduction of pollution as well as independence from fossil fuel is available in concept. So far, we have not shown enough political will to implement a solution.

As we grow in consciousness, we become more aware that our consuming as well as our producing material goods has effects beyond ourselves. We use our purchasing power wisely and beneficially by being aware of our impact on ourselves, the producers, and the whole social and natural environment. In our work-life we need to discover what the Buddhists call right livelihood. A desirable work-life leads to greater integrity and integration, the very essence of the good. We have an unprecedented capacity for destruction but also an opportunity for building the human and biotic community. A major ethical mandate for us at his stage of our evolution requires us to develop and live out a philosophical view that combines scientific and technological know-how with a reverence for our relationships with each other and with the natural world.

Consciousness and the Natural World

The practical ethical change, which our new awareness requires, belongs to a much more comprehensive change in consciousness. One of the most powerful voices in explaining the connection between consciousness and our care of the environment belongs to Thomas Berry (1914—2009). Berry devotes a chapter in his book, *The Dream of the Earth,*[111] to "Christian Spirituality and the American Experience." He cites Christianity as an example of a tradition, but his observations apply to all religious, spiritual, and philosophical traditions. He points out that every classical culture abused the land and devastated the environment. But this mistreatment did not become a major problem until technology advanced to the point that the abuse and damage became terrifying in its consequences. Now we have a need for what Berry calls "...a more intimate human association with the natural world in its evolutionary unfolding."[112] Christianity could not provide a remedy if Christians held that tradition is an unchanging body of beliefs, values, and prescribed actions, to which change would be considered heretical destruction.

Berry, however, points out that every tradition constitutes a process rather than a fixed body of ideas. When reverence toward a tradition makes change more difficult if not impossible, then the tradition becomes a big part of the problem. But if a tradition is a process, then it can and must change. As Berry states it "...traditions must constantly go beyond any existing expression of themselves to form new expressions."[113] Berry argues that Christianity must undergo one of the most significant changes in its history. This change is needed as part of a more comprehensive change in human consciousness that stems from the discovery of the evolutionary process of the universe generally, and more specially, life-forms on earth. The human body constitutes an expression of this process and so does the human mind. Evolutionary science has made us aware of the brutality of the whole process by which we humans developed, but it has also made us aware that we are biological beings who are conscious of both good and evil.

Theologian, James A. Nash, set out to develop a systematic ecological theology.[114] Nash argues that an ecological theology consists of more than a creation theology, but he logically begins with creation. The major Christian expressions of faith, the Apostle's and the Nicene Creeds, begin with the affirmation that God alone creates all things. The creation stories in Genesis Chapter 1 and Genesis Chapter 2, not only reject other deities but also reject any kind of dualism. One of the dualities that Nash mentions is the dualism of God as the Orderer versus chaotic disorder. Throughout this book I have been describing good as harmony overcoming the evil of disharmony. But my view is consistent with a non-dualistic notion of creation *ex nihilo*. If God is perfect Being, then His opposite in nothingness. I have described creation as the long process of calling created reality from nothing, through chaos, into cosmos. We humans, as we become aware that we are natural beings and develop a reverence for nature, constitute an important moment in that process.

Writing as a Christian theologian, Nash encounters the passages in Genesis in which God declares creation good. Nash sees the problem that jumps out at us when we feel the depth of evil and suffering in creation. A literal interpretation of Genesis would lay the blame for evil on the sinfulness of the first humans. But death and suffering along with most of what we consider evil presented itself from the beginning, eons before the first human. We can understand the goodness of creation, not by looking back at it as a finished product, but by looking ahead to the hoped-for outcome of the ongoing process of creation. As Nash says of creation, "It is very good because it is being brought to fulfillment by a good God."[115] Nash admits that Christian theology has often neglected the non-human world. But an understanding of the relation between God and creation, and all creatures with each other, leads Christians to a reverence for all life. Hence the title of his book, *Loving Nature.*

The outcome of any eco-theology presents the whole natural world as something to be appreciated and cared for. The implications, therefore, are both aesthetic and ethical. If the materialists were right, the natural world would be neither good nor evil, but for any living thing on earth, it appears to be extremely hostile. The materialist can legitimately question how anyone can see the world as a product of a good Creator. However, a mindful look at nature, one that affirms the priority of consciousness, can enable us to see the good emerging as the world slowly evolves from nothingness to the fulfillment of being.

Chapter 9:
Evolution and Creativity

Let us create man in our own image and likeness.

Genesis

The worldview that I have been explaining in this work sees the universe as "a process of moving from absolute chaos to a cosmos that expresses order, beauty, harmony, consciousness, freedom, joy, and love." In this chapter, I will show how our human acts of creativity manifest the good that we find in the evolutionary process of the universe. The decisive question is whether our human acts of creativity can be reduced to random events in our brains, or whether we participate in the work of the universe itself. Most of us, whether or not we believe in God as a Creator, believe that humans are creators. Human creativity bears different meaning for those whom I call materialists and those whom I call teleologists. But before examining the differences, we have to consider what we hold in common about human creativity.

Charles Sanders Pierce on Creativity

While acknowledging that many, if not most, philosophers have offered their views on creativity, my main discussion on human creativity will draw from the work of American philosopher Charles Sanders Pierce (1839 -1914). Pierce saw both evolution and creativity as expressions of the "Law of Mind." When he writes of the "mind" and "ideas," he does not limit the meaning of these terms to mere abstract intellectual entities that he refers to disdainfully as "airy nothings." Rather, he believes that, as ideas develop, they become embodied in physical reality.

According to Peirce the whole process of world formation is an expression of "The Law of Mind." According to this law, ideas are attracted to other ideas and form larger and more general ideas. These larger ideas are then attracted to other, such larger ideas to form even larger and more general ideas. A physical expression of this process shows itself as objects develop in complexity to form atoms and molecules, proteins, cells, and organisms. *Each of these steps result in an organization that is qualitatively different.* For example, the combination of hydrogen and oxygen form H20, the unlikely appearing, but qualitatively different substance, water. Thus, creation, cosmic or human, does not consist of just accumulation. Real creation involves attraction of opposites. Large chunks of ideas that may be unrelated, or even hostile, come together to form new ideas and even new worlds.

For any of us human creators, the question centers on how we face that which is foreign to us. The natural tendency on one level, the level below the mind, is to run away from or destroy that which we see as foreign. This is the usual reaction of a dog or a child. We can meet the foreign with fear, or hate, or perhaps indifference. But these attitudes are not very creative. By contrast, The Law of Mind holds that ideas have an affection for one another. The key question asks whether we can have an affection for that which is foreign. Can we love the stranger or even the enemy? Our religious traditions tell us to do so, but the issue here is not ethics, but creativity. Artists bring things together, and the creative process involves bringing things together that do not seem to get along. Can we have a loving struggle with that which is other than us and that which is opposite us? Of course we can—that ability constitutes the difference between the creator and the destroyer?

In showing a love between opposites, even though it may be a struggling love, we can begin with reason and expression—philosophy and art. This discussion, inspired by C. S. Peirce, sees *reason* as a manifestation of the *general* process of the evolution of the universe.

The term *idea* refers to this or that manifestation of *generalization*. Manifestations are individual events that are included in a general idea. According to Peirce, the very meaning of a general idea consists of governing individual events. Two momentous implications follow from this. First, an idea must be embodied to be fulfilled, and second, an idea can never be completely fulfilled. From the first point, it follows that intellectual experiences that cannot be embodied—airy nothings—do not count as real ideas of reason. From the second point we can learn that ideas are always incipient and growing. Every idea has more potential manifestations than can ever be realized.

Peirce illustrates his point with the example of human character. The character of a person consists of the ideas that a person will conceive and the effort that he or she will make if the occasion calls for it. But persons can never manifest all that is in them. They can never realize all of their potential. The full manifestation of a character would require more events than can ever occur in a lifetime. Life is always dynamic and death is always tragic because there is always more to do for fulfillment.

Through the analogy of human character, Peirce leads up to what he considers to be "the most admirable ideal," namely the development of reason. Just as the development of a human character requires more manifestation than can be realized in a lifetime, so the full development of reason involves a process of manifestations that is never finished; In Peirce's words:

> The development of Reason consists, you will observe, in embodiment, that is, in manifestation. The creation of the universe, which did not take place during a busy week in the year 4004 B. C., but is going on today and never will be done, is this very development of Reason. I do not see how one can have a more satisfying ideal of the admirable than the development of Reason so understood. [116]

Reason is the process of bringing things together. As such, it is a theological and cosmological principle and the goal of all human ethics as well as science. But most important for the purpose of this chapter, it is the principle that governs artistic creativity. Quoting Peirce again, "Under this conception, the ideal of conduct will be to execute our little function in the operation of the creation by giving a hand toward rendering the world more reasonable whenever it is up to us." [117] By doing whatever creative act each of us is capable of, we fulfill an ethical obligation and contribute to the highest ideal—the embodiment of reason.

Creativity and Connecting

While creativity may be a very complex phenomenon, there are two factors that stand out as constituting the creative activity. These are connecting things that were not previously seen as connected, and scooping from the unconscious. Both of these involve the embodiment of reason. First, let's look at the act of connecting.

When we create, we never make something from nothing; we always make something new from what we find. The new product emerges from bringing together things that had previously been separated or even opposed. As the pre-Socratic philosopher Heraclitus said, we produce new life from male and female, we produce musical harmony from high and low notes. The product of creativity may be an integration of parts that had been in opposition, or of parts that were simply lying around chaotically. In either case, the human creator brings forth a unity that includes balance, wholeness, and radiance. I will use a few examples to illustrate my theme. These examples are not systematic and are not meant to prove anything. But they will show how human creation consists of bringing diverse things together. I will begin with some examples from poetry.

Poetry

The elements of poetry consist of the words of the poet's language. Even the poet who coins new words does not create them out of raw sounds, but out of words. For example, the poet might turn a noun into a verb or vice versa. But the poet puts words together in ways they had not been put together before to express feelings, project images, tell stories, or relate ideas. One of the best examples of joining ideas that seems to be mutually opposed can be seen in Francis Thompson's "Hound of Heaven." In the first stanza, he writes:

> But with unhurrying chase
> And unperturbed pace
> Deliberate speed—majestic instancy

By joining the speedy and the deliberate, the poet creates an atmosphere and a feeling that could not be created by either one of these opposite by itself. Yet he joins them so that they fit together perfectly. I think that an almost unlimited number of examples could be found, but I will mention only two more to clarify the point.

Thomas Gray begins his "Elegy Written in a Country Churchyard:"

The Curfew tolls the knell of parting day.

We usually do not identify the end of the day with the end of a life, but by doing so, Gray is able to create a mood that we can all understand. He follows up a few lines later with. All the air a solemn stillness holds.

Perhaps for some, evening bears a new meaning after reading the poem.

One more of the many examples that could be given is found in Matthew Arnold's "Dover Beach." The opening lines say:

The sea is calm tonight
The tide is full, the moon lies fair
Upon the straits;

The reader might be expecting a nice calming verse about a leisurely life by the sea. But the poem goes on to describe "eternal sadness," "human misery," and the "melancholy, long, withdrawing roar" of "The Sea of Faith." The concluding stanza begins:

Ah love, let us be true
To one another!

The concluding lines of the poem, in stark contrast to the opening lines read:
And we are here as on a darkling plain
Swept with confused alarms of struggle and flight
Where ignorant armies clash by night.

Neither a poem about the strife and suffering of the world, nor a poem about the narrator and his love on a calm night, would have been as powerful as this surprising juxtaposition and integration. Creativity connects things that do not seem to go together.

Science

Many examples of connecting can be found in the history of scientific creativity. Like poets, creative scientists connect things that were not previously connected, or show connections that had not previously been known. One of the clearest examples can be found in Darwin's theory of evolution through natural selection. Among other elements, he connected his observation in nature with the economic theory of Thomas Malthus. Life is a struggle that not all can survive.

Other example of science advancing by making connections include; Newton connecting falling bodies with planetary movement,

Benjamin Franklin connecting lightning with electricity, Clark Maxwell connecting Michael Faraday's magnetic fields with electricity. Such examples abound and a whole history of science could be developed just by showing how scientists made connections.

Visual Art

To illustrate how painting expresses creation by connecting, I will draw on the thought of Albert Camus. In his book, *The Rebel,* Camus devotes a chapter to rebellion and art. He argues that artistic rebellion is a demand for unity and a rejection of the world as it is. Artists look at a world that is dis-unified and chaotic. Through their art they unify a subject by isolating it from the multiplicity of changing things of which it is a part. If the painting portrays an action, it isolates, in space and time, that which would have become lost by the following action.

In the current era, the role of capturing an aspect of reality in time and space may be performed by the photographer. Although there could be a long list of photographs to illustrate this point, three well-known pictures are mentioned here. These are: the hoisting of the flag at Iwo Jima, the sailor kissing the nurse in Times Square on VJ Day, and the firefighters raising an America flag amidst the destruction of "9-11." Each of these events would have happened, even if the photographer had not captured them. But not only would we not remember them, but very few, if any, would even have seen them. Marines and soldiers might have remembered that they raised American flags when they could; those who were in Times Square on VJ Day would have remembered a lot of hugging and kissing along with other celebrations. The firefighters who raised the flag on 9-11 might have remembered doing so, but that event would probably not be their dominant memory amidst the suffering and grief of that day. But the photos present permanent and unified images that enable us to make some sense out of the evil and confusion of war and terrorist attacks.

To go back to the creative work of the painter, even if the subject is something as relatively permanent as a landscape, the subject constantly changes, and certainly the human view of it changes with time and space. The artist isolates a particular view from a particular position at a particular time. The picture becomes an orderly and unified image that would otherwise disappear into its surroundings. Camus holds that the artist creates beauty by rejecting reality as it is and exalting a certain aspect of it. Artistic creation shows that humans can have an idea better than the world as we find it. But better does not mean different, it means unified.

Here, we can pick up the connection between artistic creation and the theme of this book. Artists strive to create a unity that expresses wholeness, integration, and thereby some good aspect of our constantly changing reality. The expression often, but not always, takes the form of beauty. But even if the emotion evoked is something such as horror rather than aesthetic enjoyment, the goodness remains the theme. For example, Goya's painting "The Third of May," showing French soldiers executing Spanish villagers, cannot be called beautiful in any ordinary sense of the word. A viewer does not look at the painting to experience joy. But the painting preserves the memory of the tragedy and of the victims who would otherwise be forgotten. Goodness is expressed by its absence in the suffering of the Spanish and in the brutality of the French, who were supposed to be enlightened. Our awareness of the evil and the missing human connection between the Spanish villagers and the French soldiers takes a step toward the redemption of a fallen world.

Whether artistic creativity expresses beauty, tragedy, or any other human experience, it holds a different meaning for the materialist and the teleologist. For the materialist, the good that shines in the creative act constitutes a brief glimpse of light, valued by some humans, but not bearing much significance in the realm of cosmic reality. For the teleologist, human creativity stands out as part of the universal narrative in which the whole cosmos becomes slowly connected until it expresses a beauty and order beyond what we can easily imagine. Musicians, poets, painters, scientists, and other creative artists catch a glimpse of higher reality and make it partially available to the rest of us.

Creation as Scooping from the Unconscious

In addition to the connection of opposites as a theme of creativity, another major theme is reaching into the unconscious. The German word for creator is *Schopfer,* a term that connotes one who scoops from a well. The book of Genesis describes the Spirit of God hovering over the waters. But in the case of human creativity, creators scoop into their unconscious. A powerful example of human creativity describing an idea of divine creativity can be found in Franz Joseph Haydn's "Creation Oratorio." In German, the oratorio's name is "Die Schopfung," literally the scooping, figuratively the creation. Haydn quotes from Genesis, and the English translation reads: "The Spirit of God hovered over the waters and God said 'Let there be light.'" The music up to this point is solemn, slow, and quiet. The next line proclaims "And there was light." Now the music is loud, exciting, and joyful. Creation involves surprise. There is an unexpected uniting of opposites—light and darkness, consciousness and the unconscious.

To the extent that creativity entails reaching into the unconscious, we can ask whether this action implies a reality better than or worse than the world of the conscious mind. A Freudian view holds that creative work dredges up thoughts and desires of sex and violence that the conscious mind suppresses. In fact, the themes of sex and violence often show up in poetry, drama, literature, and, perhaps to a lesser degree, in painting. So if the materialists are right, the cosmos does not make sense, but we humans can have our moments in which we create or appreciate a fleeting moment of significance. We can find these moments in different forms in science and in art.

Artistic creativity takes on a very different meaning if we assume the teleological attitude. We can begin our discussion of the teleological position where we left off with the materialist position—with Freud. For Freud, *Eros*—love, represents integration, while *Thanatos*—death, represents disintegration. As I have argued throughout this book, these two forces are found throughout the cosmos and in human experience. Art that express Eros embodies the integrating force of the universe, while art that embodies Thanatos expresses our attempts to overcome or to redeem particular forms of disintegration.

The teleological view affirms an erotic force in nature working to integrate the parts, which by themselves tend to disintegration. To use the example of painters, when they produce beauty, they are tapping into an ever-present reality that most of us miss most of the time. The beauty can be found in a human face or form, in a landscape, or in a design. The consciousness of the painter moves to a deeper level of awareness and enables us to follow. The penetrating to deeper levels stands out even more dramatically in the art of the musical composer. Those of us who are not composers cannot have a first-hand knowledge of that which composers experience. But by listening to the music we can gain some degree of entrance to a world beyond our ordinary experience

Materialists and teleologists can agree on the obvious fact of the reality of human creativity. Further, this fact does not prove that one view or the other is true. But from the teleological view, human creativity is a matter of course. If there is a creative power in or over the universe, it presumably surpasses the current state of physical and biological evolution. But what if creatures such as human beings on earth are moving to where they can catch glimpses of the higher reality? This is what human creators seem to do. People whom we refer to by the term "genius," such as Raphael, Mozart, and Einstein, experience an order, beauty, and integrity that they express as a painting, a symphony, or a physical theory. This can be said of any creative artist, scientist, or person working in fields in which they produce something good that was not there before.

So if my hypothesis is correct, we belong to a narrative that is over 13 billion years old and in which warring elements are being led from all-in-division to a community characterized by integration, beauty, and goodness. This process continues on earth as biological evolution, and in the human race, in the development of consciousness. The most creative among us, whether they be scientists, poets, painters, or musicians, take an especially active part in this process and show the way to the rest of us. An aesthetic experience gives us a glimpse of what is possible.

Endnotes

[1] Brian L. Silver, *The Ascent of Science* (Oxford University Press, 1918), 234.

[2] Plato has Socrates criticizing the philosopher Anaxagoras for affirming Mind as the cause of the universe and still attributing the order of the universe to material things instead of to the Mind. *Phaedo* in *Plato: The Collected Dialogues* edited by Edith Hamilton and Huntington Cairns (Princeton university press, 1961), 79-80.

[3] Thomas Nagel, *Mind and Cosmos* (Oxford University Press, 2012.) Nagel argues against the materialist view, but points out that materialism is so prevalent in our contemporary secular culture, that many people will find doubts about it to be outrageous.

[4] The term "the Good" will be used to describe all that we may consider to be good before attempting any definition or limitation of the term.

[5] Aristotle, *Nicomachaen Ethics,* in *The Basic Works of Aristotle*, edited by Richard McKeon, (New York: Random House, 1941), 935.

[6] St. Thomas, *Summa Theologica I –II,* Question 91, article 2, in Introduction *to Thomas Aquinas,* edited by Anton Pegis, (New York: The modern Library, Random House, 1948), 618.

[7] Francis Crick. *The Astonishing Hypothesis: The Scientific Search for the Soul* (New York: Simon and Schuster Touchstone Book, 1995) p. 3.

[8] Daniel C. Dennett, *Freedom Evolves* (New York: Penguin Books, 2003), 5

[9] Richard Dawkins, *The Selfish Gene.* (Oxford University Press, 1989), 201.

[10]Jean-Paul Sartre, *Being and Nothingness,* translated by Hazel Barnes (New York: Washington Square Press, 1953), 46.

[11] Christof Koch defines a miracle as an intrusion into the physical world from outside, an event that would violate the principle of conservation of energy. I am not asserting that miracles of this type take place. Nor am I denying that some "miraculous" events might occur in ways that are beyond the understanding of contemporary science.

[12] Charles Sanders Peirce, (CP 6.287). *Collected Papers,* Cambridge: Harvard University Press in the Electronic Version, InteLex Corporation.

[13] Dawkins, 198.

[14] Josiah Royce, *The Problem of Christianity* (Washington, D.C. : The Catholic University of America Press, 2001), 62.

[15] Alfred Tennyson, "In Memoriam."

[16] Daniel Dennett offers a materialist explanation for consciousness and freedom in his works *Consciousness Explained and Freedom Evolve.* Chapter 4 of this book examines his arguments.

[17] Stephen Hawking and Leonard Mlodinow, *The Grand Design* (New York, Bantam Books, 2010), 34.

[18] James Gleick, *Chaos: Making A New Science* (New York: Penguin Books, 1987), 8.

[19] Kenneth R. Miller, *Finding Darwin's God* (New York: Harper Collins Publishers, 1999), 189. Miller observes that Phillip Johnson, a denier of evolution, and Richard Lewontin, a strict materialist, agree that belief in evolution and belief in God are incompatible. Miller writes: "The giddy irony of this situation is that intellectual opposites like Johnson and Lewontin actually find themselves in a symbiotic relationship—-each insisting vigorously that evolution implies an absolute materialism that is not compatible with religion."

[20] Daniel Dennett, *Freedom Evolves* (New York: Penguin Books, 2003), 31.

[21] Hawking and Mlodinow, 179.

[23] No one can think of nothingness, because if there were nothing, there would be no

thinking. We may not be able to go as far as Descartes and posit a thinking substance – *res cogitans* – but we could not deny that there *is* thinking.

[24] Ernest Becker, *The Denial of Death* (New York: The Free Press: A Division of

Macmillan, 1973), 281. Becker does not conclude that evolution has no meaning, only that we cannot comprehend it. He writes "Life seems to expand in an unknown direction for an unknown purpose." 286.

[25] John F. Haught, *God After Darwin* (Boulder, Colorado: Westview Press, 2000) 114.

[26] Teilhard de Chardin, *The Phenomenon of Man* (New York: Harper & Row, 1959) 313.

[27] Haught quotes Whitehead, 107

[28] MacBeth, Act V Scene 5. *The Complete Works of Shakespeare,* 882.

[29] Haught, *God After Darwin* 111.

[30] Haught, *God After Darwin, 112.*

[31] Haught, 41

[32] Haught, 42

[33] Miller. In chapters 3,4 and 5.

[34] Miller makes it clear that in calling evolution a theory, he is not denying the fact that living things evolved. Evolution by natural

selection, or "descent with modification," is a theory in that it provides science with a method to account for how evolution happens.

[35] Among contemporaries who hold to a materialism that reject any other explanation Miller cites: Douglas Futyuma, Richard Dawkins, Daniel Dennett, Edward O. Wilson, and Richard Lewontin.

[36] This statement does not exhaust the intellectual and spiritual richness of the age called the Enlightenment. Charles Taylor, for one, documents the flowering of ethical insight that accompanied the belief known as Darwinism. Charles Taylor, *A Secular Age* (Cambridge, Massachusetts: The Belknap Press of Harvard University press, 20007) Chapter 6, "Providential Deism."

[37] The thoughts summarized in the preceding two paragraphs are argued cogently by David Miller in *Finding Darwin's God* in Chapter Seven, "Beyond Materialism."

[38] "Is Life Worth Living?" in *The Will to Believe and Other Essays in Popular Philosophy* (New York: Dover Publications, 1956), 61.

[39] James did not live long enough to benefit from the development of process theology and philosophy, but his religious insights would have found some support from the Process theologians. One good example of the compatibility of James and process theology, an example that does not mention James, is: Mark Johnston. *Saving God: Religion After Idolatry* (Princeton University Press, 2009) Especially Chapter 8, "Process Panentheism."

[40] Even today we know that the sun is a cause, in the sense of a necessary condition, of life on Earth.

[41] Plato, *The Republic,* 6:505 In *Plato: The Collected Dialogues* edited by Edith Hamilton and Huntington Cairns (Princeton University Press, 1961), *740.*

[42] Aristotle, *The Nicomachaen Ethics,* 1094:1, in *The Basic Works of Aristotle* edited by Richard Mckeon (New York: Random House, 1941), 935.

[43] Timothy Radcliffe, 0. P., *What is the Point of Being a Christian?* (New York: Burns and Oates, 2006) Chapter 6.

[44] I do not have source for this argument, but I have often heard it from students as well as from educated adults. I assume the reader has heard this one too.

[45] William James, *Principles of Psychology Volume II* (New York, Dover Publications, 1950), 561.

[46] The issue of "grace" was deliberately left out of this discussion, because the point is that free will constitutes a necessary condition for doing good rather that being the source of evil in the world. This hold true regardless of anyone's theological belief as to whether grace is necessary for a good action.

[47] Michael A. Susko, *Ten Pulses of Evolution* (AllrOneofUs Publishing, 2020). Susko argues, with strong evidence from fossil finds and chemical analysis, that evolution takes place with surprising quantitative leaps rather than in a gradual linear way. He identifies ten "nodes" in each of which there is a remarkable increase in consciousness, mobility, and social connection.

[48] Leonard Mladinow, *The Drunkard's Walk.* (New York: Random House, 2009), 217.

[49] William James, *The Will to Believe and Other Essays in Popular Philosophy* (New York: Dover Publications, 1956), 51.

[50] Ibid., 53.

[51] John Haught, *God After Darwin* (Boulder ,Colorado: Westview Press, 2000), 126.

[52] Haught 126-130.

[53] Haught 128.

[54] Susko, *Ten Pulses*. Susko shows that the pulses toward greater consciousness, mobility, and social connection occur in increasingly shorter intervals. Evolutionary time is logarithmic, meaning that, in this case, the intervals between the nodes become exponentially shorter. For instance, the first node, the appearance of life on earth occurred 4 billion years ago. The next mode was 2 billion years ago, the third, 1 billion years ago. To jump to the ninth mode, the appearance of hominoids, that happened 15,7 million years ago; humans appeared in the tenth node, 7.8 million years ago.

[55] Andrew Newberg and Eugene D'Aquili, *Why God Won't go Away*. (New York:

Ballantine Books, 2001). The authors describe the neuro-science behind such

experience, but leave as an open question whether these experiences involve reality or a merely subjective state.

[56] William James, *Principles of Psychology Vol I* (New York: Dover Publications, 1950), 186. After examining several terms used by his contemporaries, James chooses to use the terms "thought" and "feelings." He prefers to use them interchangeably to describe our conscious states, but warns of the problem that some readers might think of feelings as only sensations and of thoughts as only abstractions.

[57] William James, *Essays in Radical Empiricism and A Pluralistic Universe*

(Gloucester MA: Peter Smith, 1967), 304.

[58] William James, *A Pluralistic Universe,* 305 -306. James credits Martin Luther for being the first to effectively "break the crust of naturalistic self-sufficiency." Luther attributed the insight to Saint Paul.

[59] *A Pluralistic Universe,* 307.

[60] William James, *Varieties of Religious Experience* (New York: New American Library), *298*.

[61] Christof Koch, *Consciousness: Confession of a Romantic Reductionist.* (Cambridge, Massachusetts: The MIT Press, 2012) 6.

[62] Koch, 8.

[63] Koch, 26.

[64] Koch, 27.

[65] Koch., 39.

[66] Koch, 42.

[67] Koch, 92.

[68] Koch, 104-105. Koch cites an experiment performed by Benjamin Libet at the
University of California at San Francisco in the early 1980s. He affirms that the experiment has been repeated and refined and the results still stand.

[69] Koch, 93.

[70] Koch, 111.

[71] Koch, 119.

[72] Koch, 119.

[73] Koch, 132. I think that this statement is obviously true, but Koch confirms it speaking of his conversations, presumably including scientists.

[74] Koch, 125.

[75] Koch, 126. Koch expresses the debt of gratitude that he and Francis Crick owe to Giuoli Tononi for the concept of *integrated information.*

[76] Koch, 133.

[77] Koch, 135.

[78] Koch, 162.

[79] Koch, 165.

[80] Koch, 165.

[81] Richard Holmes, *The Age of wonder* (New York: Pantheon Books, 2008), 167.

[82] Rudolph Otto, *The Idea of the Holy* (New York: Oxford University Press, Paperback, 1985) Chapters 4, 6, 15. This brief comment about attributing consciousness to inanimate objects does not speak for the whole history of animism across cultures. It does not even express the complexity of Otto's thought about the connection between animism and the development of religion.

[83] G, S. Kirk and J. E. Raven, *The Presocratic Philosophers* (Cambridge: The

University Press,1963) 171.

[84] *Plato*: *The Collected Dialogues* edited by Edith Hamilton and Huntington Cairns (Princeton University Press), 1162.

[85] Metaphysics Book XII, Chapter 7, in *The Basic Works of Aristotle,* edited by Richard McKeon, (New York: Random House, 1966), 880.

[86] Since the term "rational" is used several times here, some clarification may be helpful. Most readers know what rational means, and writers often use the term as if its meaning were self-evident, or at least common knowledge. It is hard to define "rational" without going in a circle of synonyms. I offer this clarification. A rational view of reality goes beyond the immediacy of perception and images, and allows us to comprehend generalizations that include many percepts or images, and enables us to be aware of how things are connected, especially in terms of causation.

[87] Nicomachean Ethics, Book X, Chapter 6, in McKeon, 1104.

[88] "On the Soul , Book III, Chapter 5, in McKeon, 592.

[89] Amos 5: 21, 22, 24, 8: 4.

[90] Josiah Royce, *The Problem of Christianity* (Washington, D.C., The Catholic University of America Press, 2001), 307.

[91] Daniel Berrigan, *Isaiah: Spirit of Courage, Gift of Tears* (Minneapolis: Fortress Press, 1996), 9.

[92] Berrigan, 10.

[93] The phrase, "bodily-based individualism," should not be interpreted as a negative attitude toward the body. The theme throughout this work has been that the tension in the world is not based on two levels of reality e.g., physical and spiritual. Rather it is based on conflicting processes. Creative evolution leads to greater integrity and integration. But there is a tendency for things to fall back into nothingness – to disintegrate. So, a healthy body must resist the disintegrating tendency of disease and death. At the social level, the person can contribute to the care and integration of the community with bodily actions. But our bodies are what individuate us, so we have to be aware of the tendency to give in to anything that disrupts the integrity of the community.

[94] John Haught, *Science and Faith* (Mahwah, NJ: Paulist Press, 2012), 30 -34.

[95] Sean Carroll, *The Big Picture* (New York: Dutton, 2017), 31.

[96] A clear example of how training and practice can lead a scientist to disdain questions that cannot be answered by empirical verification can be seen in an article written by Thomas Edison: "I have never seen the slightest scientific proof of the religious theories of heaven and hell, of future life for individuals, or of a personal God. I earnestly believe that I am right...Proof! Proof! That is what I have always been after; that is what my mind requires before it can accept

a theory as fact." Quoted in Edmund Morris, *Edison* (New York: Random House, 2020), 104.

[97] William James, "The Energies of Men" in *The Moral Equivalent of War and Other Essays* edited by John K. Roth (Harper and Row Publishers, 1970), 48.

[98] Ken Wilbur, editor, *Quantum Questions: Mystical Writings of the World's Greatest Physicists* (Boston: Shambhala Publications, 2001). Wilbur has shown that most of the seminal scientific thinkers of the twentieth century acknowledge that science cannot answer the metaphysical questions, but that their study of science motivated them to go beyond the limits of science to explore the meaning of reality. In this chapter, I am trying to understand and support the materialists, not quarrel with them.

[99] Carroll, 3-4.

[100] Thomas Merton, *Journals Vol 2, Entering the Silence – Becoming a Monk* (San Francisco: Harper, 1996), 150.

[101] Michael Ruse, *On Purpose* (Princeton, New Jersey: Princeton University Press,2018). Michael Ruse is the author of more than fifty books, and I am limiting my discussion to the contents of this one.

[102] Ruse, 178.

[103] In his well-known work, *Leviathan,* Hobbes argues that in a state of nature the only law is survival, and every person is an enemy to every other. Civilization can develop only if there is an overwhelming power to keep the peace.

[104] I express my understanding on social justice in *Ethics and the Full-Breasted Richness of Life* (AllrOne of Us Publishing, 2020). Some of the material used here is taken directly from the earlier book.

[105] It is not my intention here to present the history of Romanticism or to trace the love of nature before that time. My purpose is to point out that Environmental Ethics developed for the

most part in the second half of the twentieth century and that it is compatible with the theme of this work.

[106] Aldo Leopold , "The Land Ethic" in *Environmental Ethics: What Really Matters, What Really Works,* edited by David Schmidtz and Elizabeth Willott (New York: Oxford University Press, 2002), 28.

[107] ST 1, 48 ad. 2, cited in Larry Rasmussen, *Earth Community/ Earth Ethics* (New York: Orbis Books, Maryknoll, 1996), 193.

[108] E. F. Schumacher, *A Guide for the Perplexed* (New York: Harper and Row, 1977), 134.

[109] Wendell Berry, *"The Gift of Good Land* (New York: North Point Press, Farrar, Straus, and Giroux, 1982), 178.

[110] Wendell Berry, *The Gift of Good Land,* 274-275. Theologian, Ellen Davis author of *Scripture, Culture, and Agriculture: An Agrarian Reading of the Bible,* (New York: Cambridge University Press, 2009) with an introduction by Wendell Berry, is developing theological insights compatible with Berry's work.

[111] Thomas Berry, *The Dream of the Earth* (San Francisco: Sierra Club Books, 1988).

[112] Berry, 116

[113] Berry, 117

[114] James A. Nash, *Loving Nature: Ecological Integrity and Christian Responsibility* (Nashville: Abingdon Press, 1991).

[115] Nash, 100.

[116] Charles Sanders Pierce, *Collected Papers* (Cambridge: Harvard University Press Electronic Version Intelex Corp.) CP 1.615.

[117] CP 1.615.

Did you love *The Problem of Good: Finding Purpose Amid the Chaos of Reality*? Then you should read *The Neglected Doctrine of the Holy Spirit: Josiah Royce as a Guide to Renewing Theology*[1] by Richard Mullin!

[2]

The Holy Spirit is a dimension of Godhood which is not given much attention, yet one that is critical for our spiritual development. In this work Richard Mullin shows how the contribution of American Philosophers at the turn of the 20th century can serve as a basis to reenvision theology. Importantly, he distinguishes the historical church with all its shortcomings and the Universal or "Beloved Community." Read this work if you are seeking a mature spiritual vision and one for which the church is a task that remains to be completed.

Read more at https://www.letphilosophyshine.com/.

---

1. https://books2read.com/u/3k51zO

2. https://books2read.com/u/3k51zO

About the Author

Richard P. Mullin earned his PhD, in philosophy and taught philosophy at St. Bernard College in Cullman, Alabama for seven years and at Wheeling Jesuit University for thirty years. He also taught Business Ethics in the MBA program at Wheeling Jesuit. He has lectured in American philosophy in Slovenia and Slovakia and frequently read papers at the meetings of the Society for the Advancement of American Philosophy. In *The Soul of Classical American Philosophy: The Ethical and Spiritual Insights of William James, Josiah Royce, and Charles Sanders Pierce (SUNY Press2007)*, he portrays the governing ideas of the founders of American Pragmatism. Previous books from AllrOneofUs Publishing: *Ethics and the Full-Breasted Richness of Life: A Roycean Approach to Nourishing the Good,* and *The Neglected Doctrine of the Holy Spirit: Josiah Royce's Christian Doctrine of Life as a Guide to Renewing Theology.*

Read more at https://www.letphilosophyshine.com/.

9 798201 503758